Prayer

Also by Matthew Fox

Prayer

A Radical Response to Life

Matthew Fox

originally published as
On Becoming a Musical, Mystical Bear

Jeremy P. Tarcher/Penguin
a member of
Penguin Group (USA) Inc.
New York

Most Tarcher/Putnam books are available at special quantity discounts for bulk purchase for sales promotions, premiums, fund-raising, and educational needs. Special books or book excerpts also can be created to fit specific needs. For details, write Putnam Special Markets, 375 Hudson Street, New York, NY 10014.

Jeremy P. Tarcher/Penguin
a member of
Penguin Group (USA) Inc.
375 Hudson Street
New York, NY 10014
www.penguin.com

First published in 1972 by Paulist Press
First Jeremy P. Tarcher/Putnam Edition 2001
Copyright © 1972, 1976 by Matthew Fox
Introduction © 2001 by Matthew Fox

Acknowledgment is gratefully given to Harcourt Brace Jovanovich, Inc., publishers, for permission to cite from T. S. Eliot's "Little Gidding" and from e. e. cummings' Introduction to his *New Poems* and "A Poet's Advice to Students." The epigraph is from "Portrait of a Lady" in *Collected Poems 1909–1962* by T. S. Eliot, copyright 1936 by Harcourt Brace Jovanovich, Inc.; copyright © 1963, 1964, by T. S. Eliot. Reprinted by permission of Harcourt Brace Jovanovich, Inc. Excerpts from *The Jerusalem Bible*, copyright © 1966 by Darton, Longman & Todd, Ltd. and Doubleday & Company, Inc. Used by permission of the publisher. Richard Farina's "Birmingham Sunday" is used by permission of the publisher, Ryerson Music Publishers, Inc. © 1965, all rights reserved.

Library of Congress Cataloging-in-Publication Data
Fox, Matthew, date.
    Prayer : a radical response to life / by Matthew Fox.
      p. cm.
    Rev. ed. of: On becoming a musical, mystical bear. ©1976.
    Includes bibliographical references.
    ISBN 1-58542-098-0
    1. Prayer—Christianity. 2. Spirituality. I. Fox, Matthew, date. On becoming a musical, mystical bear. II. Title.
BV210.2 .F69   2001   2001018912
248.4—dc21

Printed in the United States of America

10 9 8 7 6 5 4

To Javier Garcia Lemus, Aaron Lane, Chad Ghosthorse, Julia Butterfly, and other young mystic-prophets who are generous in their radical response to life and its beauties and are not afraid to do battle with life's enemies, knowing that time is short.

Perhaps it is not too late. . . .
And I must borrow every changing shape
To find expression . . . dance, dance
Like a dancing bear
                                    T. S. Eliot

Contents

Prayer

PREFACE TO THE 2001 EDITION

As I begin this preface for a book I wrote thirty years ago, I must offer a personal confession: I had not read this book in years. I approached the rereading of it in preparation for this new edition with some trepidation: Would I be embarrassed? Was it all so dated as to be immature and unusable for a new century and a new millennium? Had my subsequent writing or that of others rendered this book dated and unnecessary?

Yet I was hugely surprised on rereading it. I loved the book all over again. I took copious notes. I was moved by it and struck by how much of my subsequent writing and work was seeded in this book. I have never forsaken its basic understanding of prayer as a radical response to life and the healthy dialectic between mysticism (enjoying life) and prophecy (fighting necrophilia or those forces of injustice and oppression which interfere with life). Indeed, so much of my life has been dedicated to trying to teach and walk this understanding of spirituality.

Themes introduced in this book that have become integral to my subsequent spiritual path and teaching include the following: work as job versus work as sacred vocation (the basis of our Doctor of Ministry program at the University of Creation Spirituality, and the basis of my *The Reinvention of Work*); evil—its mystery and our need to wrestle with it (the basis of my *Sins of the Spirit*,

Blessings of the Flesh: Lessons for Transforming Evil in Soul and Society); original grace, original blessing (the basis of my *Original Blessing*); letting go (so basic in Eckhart's work, whom I discovered after this book was published); natural versus tactical ecstasies (the basis of my *Whee! We, Wee All the Way Home: Toward a Sensual, Prophetic Spirituality*); panentheism (all in God and God in all) versus theism (God out there); the call for revitalized forms of worship (which is now incarnated in our Techno Cosmic Masses, where we borrow from rave culture and replace pew sitting with trance dancing, preaching with images projected on screens); the spiritual warrior (that power in us that gives us the courage to stand up for what we believe; this theme, so universal in spiritual traditions around the world, forms the last chapter in my most recent book, *One River, Many Wells*); universality of religious truth and interfaith dialogue (the theme of the previously mentioned book on deep ecumenism); the healthy role of anger and outrage and their relation to love and warriorhood and prophecy (common to my treatment of the chakras in *Sins of the Spirit, Blessings of the Flesh* and to the treatment of prophecy in *Original Blessing*); art's primal role in spirituality, or as this book puts it, "art is more spiritual than dogma" and all persons are artists, a theme developed in our pedagogy at our University of Creation Spirituality, where art as meditation is required of all (and found in most all of my subsequent works, but especially in *Illuminations of Hildegard of Bingen,* and the work on Thomas Aquinas, *Sheer Joy,* and Meister Eckhart, *Passion for Creation*); and a call to a more horizontal and less vertical social structuring (mirrored in my call for moving from "Climbing Jacob's Ladder to Dancing Sara's Circle" in *A Spirituality Named Compassion: Uniting Mystical Awareness with Social Justice*).

Seeing this book anew and its primal place in my own intellectual evolution alerts me to truth very dear to my heart: One reason why young artists and thinkers need to be supported by elders and the greater community is because their entrance onto the scene of adulthood is a great gift from the spirit. It is meaningful to me that at the very time I am looking back to this, my first work on spirituality, I am also welcoming into my home two young artists who have not been able to afford a place to do their painting. These young men, just the age I was when I was writing *Prayer: A Radical Response to Life* (originally entitled *On Becoming a Musical, Mystical Bear*), hold great promise, and they need and deserve the support of elders. How easy it is to forget what a seamless journey we are often on and what we write or paint at sixty is not at all unrelated to what we set out to do, with vision galore and an openness to spirit and truth, in our twenties. How sad to realize how many twenty-year-olds can easily get caught up in the superficial and addictive/compulsive ways of our society and then lose their call to contribute radically to the greater community.

Allow me to say a word about the original title of this book, *On Becoming a Musical, Mystical Bear: Spirituality American Style*. I was initially planning to call the book "Spirituality American Style," when I received a significant dream in the midst of writing it. That dream was of a bear—he was big and powerful, and he was dancing and celebrating. It was a healing dream, a healing bear, and I just knew that it contained something essential to the teaching in the book. Just before the book went to publication, I read a couplet from T. S. Eliot and managed to sneak it into the text at the last second. It moved me then; it moves me still today:

> Perhaps it is not too late. . . .
> And I must borrow every changing shape
> To find expression . . . dance, dance
> Like a dancing bear

What moved me so much then was the phrase "perhaps it is not too late," for I felt—and many of my contemporaries in the sixties felt—that it *might be too late*, that the world as so many knew it and counted on it was indeed coming to an end. Some responded by drugging out; some by violence, blowing up buildings and military institutions; some by going to prison like the Berrigan brothers. But a dancing bear had encouraged me to write a book; I was borrowing a changing shape even though theologians didn't usually write books with bears in the title. But my generation had to do things—including theological things—differently. That I knew. An era was coming to an end.

Today, too, we are threatened with so much—the warming of our globe is just the latest in a series of cries of agony from Mother Earth, whom we are destroying with such abandon. When will it all stop? Is it too late? Lester Brown of the Worldwatch Institute says we have ten years left to change our ways as a species—we will not be able to undo the damage to our planet after these ten years. Thus the phrase "perhaps it is not too late" carries added weight to all our moral decisions and spiritual development at this moment in human and planetary history.

Only after the book appeared did I learn an ancient Native American story: that the earliest form of worship on this continent of "Turtle Island" was that of the bear. The bear represented the human because he stood on two legs—but he also represented the divine because he was so powerful and such a healer. What better image, then, for a book about healing and redemption of the American soul than an image of a musical, mystical bear? Was this a Christ-image for our culture? By trusting my dreams I had been led back to my childhood when Native American spirits had often spoken to me through dreams.

One problem in our culture is that neither capitalism nor rationalism entertains the child—the colorful, living, bleeding, wondering, crying, dancing imaginations of our souls is nearly enough in my opinion. Play is as necessary for spirituality as it is for sexuality (and they can be the same). Indeed, Aquinas says the nearest thing to contemplation is play.[1] And Norman O. Brown believes that "what the great world needs, of course, is a little more Eros and less strife; but the intellectual world needs it just as much."[2] To speak of play and Eros is to speak of wisdom itself, who wants to "play in the universe." (Proverbs 8. 30f.) There lies a subtle connection between theology as overly rationalistic and theology as ideology, between nonrecognition of the artistic and childlike substratum of our spiritual existence and the felt need to control others. Inquisitors make lousy baby-sitters.

At the time in my life and in our culture's life when I wrote this book, it was necessary to begin trusting one's dreams more and our institutions less. Our institutions were dying all around us. Vietnam was pitting family against family, children against parents, people against their elected officials, church members against church members. (One person I met subsequently told me the story of how one father said to his son: "Either join the army and fight in Vietnam and come home in a coffin or leave the family entirely." The young man left his family, all seven brothers and sisters, got conscientious objector status, and became an orderly in a hospital. Years later, when his son died at forty-one of AIDS, his father wept in my arms and said: "My son was right. He was more moral than I. He stood up against the Vietnam war." This story was not an isolated one.)

Student riots of the late sixties brought down governments and brought out the police, from Berkeley, California, to Madison,

1. Matthew Fox, *Sheer Joy: Conversations with Thomas Aquinas on Creation Spirituality* (San Francisco: HarperSanFrancisco, 1992), 79f.
2. Norman O. Brown, *Life Against Death* (Middletown, Conn: Wesleyan University Press, 1972), 322.

Wisconsin, to Paris, France (where I was studying and where the students literally brought down the de Gaulle goverment), to Trier, Germany (where I participated in an international gathering of young Dominicans who challenged the Order to profoundly change its ways). Liberation theologians like Gustavo Gutierrez and Jose Miranda in Latin America were announcing more prophetic dimensions to Christianity's history. Novelist John Updike talked of those times as a period "that visits mankind between millennia, between the death and rebirth of gods, when there is nothing to steer by but sex and stoicism and the stars."[3]

Feminist theologians were soon raising questions of language and God-talk and the relationship of matter and spirit. Fear of women in Christian history is based on two propositions: 1) Women represent "matter," or the flesh, and 2) matter is evil. By destroying the latter proposition you liberate spirituality from its idealistic, neo-Platonic flights from creation and from its chauvinism.

I now have a vocabulary for understanding the *context* in which this book was written: The sixties witnessed the collapse of the modern era and the opening up to the postmodern era. We didn't have words for it then—only deep feelings on both sides of the divide and a lot of action and a lot of spirit. The civil rights movement, the anti-war movement, the Student Democratic movement, the gay and lesbian movement, the feminist movement, the ecological movement—all these bore the marks of the signs of the times that we were witnesses to.

As a young Dominican, well schooled in an intellectual tradition that ran from Aristotle to Thomas Aquinas and beyond, and practicing a seven-hundred-year-old spiritual tradition of contemplation-action that included much meditation, mantra-chanting (especially

3. John Updike, *Couples* (New York: Alfred A. Knopf, 1968), 372.

the rosary), liturgical chanting of the divine office, fasting, community living, vows of poverty, celibacy, and obedience, and a strong rite of passage at the age of twenty years, I was not without tools to connect to the rising interest in spirituality and its relationship to politics. As I indicate in this book, art was the special language for expressing the mystical *and* the prophetic—the influence of the Bob Dylans and Joan Baezes and others of this period bear testimony to that. There was a political and an artistic awakening going on simultaneously. One fed the other. Prophecy fed mysticism and mysticism prophecy. Norman O. Brown put it this way: "Art seduces us into the struggle against repression."[4] The artist then *is* the mystic and the prophet, the lover and the warrior, the genuinely prayerful person. And that means each of us.

Basic to this book and to my entire vocation as a theologian and activist has been the distinction between the two streams of spirituality in the West; a distinction named for me by the great French Dominican, M. D. Chenu (who is also grandfather of liberation theology), in my studies with him in 1968 in Paris. That is, the distinction between Creation Spirituality and Fall/Redemption Spirituality. In my original preface for the paperback edition of this book in 1976, I listed the differences in the following manner (with modest adjustments here):

FALL/REDEMPTION	CREATION SPIRITUALITY
Greek	Hebrew
Spiritual means immaterial	Spiritual means what is life-giving

4. Brown, *Life Against Death*, 64.

From Plato via Augustine and Denis the Pseudo-Areopagite	From the Jews via the prophets and Jesus
Soul wars with body (Augustine)	Soul loves the body (Eckhart)
Matter is sinful or at most tolerated	Matter, too, is God-made and holy
Limit pleasure, shun it	Ecstasy is gift of Creator
Private (God and me)[5]	Political (God and us)
Centered around the theological theme of Fall and humankind's need for redemption	Centered on the theological theme of Creation: how it is good, how we say thank you by enjoying and sharing the enjoyment of it
Pride and lust are capital sins to be put to death by mortifications	Developing your talents is the Creator's desire (as in the parable of the talents). Any ascetic practices are strictly means, not ends
Negative toward the human person and human history	Affirmative toward the person and human history not in a naive optimistic sense, but in

5. Jeb Stuart Magruder, one of the principles in the Watergate episode in American Nixonian history, confesses that "we had private morality but no public morality." (Jeb Stuart Magruder, *An American Life: One Man's Road to Watergate* [New York: Antheneum, 1974], 349).

	the sense that humankind has responsibility for creation to the extent that it respects and receives the gifts and beauties of the Creator as sacred
Artists must choose between sacred and secular subjects, between spiritual and material	Every experience of beauty is an experience of God and all artistic expression is a sharing in an image and likeness of the Creator
Humankind's relationship to God is primarily vertical: God is up, humankind below. God as theistic	Humankind's relationship to God is horizontal and concentric in its meeting places. God is all in all and all is in God. God as pantheistic

The methodology of this book, in my opinion, still holds true. That is, the essence of religion is spirituality and the essence of spirituality is how we understand and practice prayer. Prayer lies at the center of spirituality as Friedrich Heiler puts it: "Prayer is the heart and center of all religion; not in dogmas and institutions, not in rites and ethical ideas, but in prayer do we grasp the peculiar quality of the religious life."[6] That which distinguishes a religious institution from other service institutions is its claim to prayer.

This book challenges the reader to grow up when it comes to prayer. A thirty-seven-year-old businessman and father of seven

6. Friedrich Heiler, *Prayer: A Study in the History and Psychology of Religion*, trans. Samuel McComb (New York: Oxford University Press, 1958), xv.

said to me years ago: "I know that I still pray like I did when I was a child. Surely there must be such a thing as an adult way of praying? How can I pass on an adult faith to my teenaged son?" A study of the prayer of Roman Catholic seminarians found that these twenty-three-year-old young men held notions on prayer identical to schoolboys aged twelve to fourteen, talking to God, for example, as if he (always he) were a superego in the sky.[7] Is religion prepared to serve adults at all? What about the "spiritual meat" versus "spiritual milk" motif of the Letter to the Hebrews or Paul's confession that when he was child he thought and believed as a child but having become a man he put away childish thinking to believe like an adult? Perhaps to learn to *unpray* may prove the first step for adult believers to return to the simple questions: What does prayer mean to us? How do we pray as adults? Where is prayer happening in our culture? Who is actually praying? Shortly before his untimely death, I received a letter from Thomas Merton that said: "The prejudice in some Catholic quarters against mysticism is a bit strange, when outside the Church there is such an intense and ill-regulated hunger and curiosity about spiritual experience (what with LSD and all that)." In this book, I reintroduce mysticism and its counterpart, prophecy, as constituting the core of prayerfulness.

I define prayer herein as *a radical response to life* wherein "radical" (from the word "root") indicates our mystical roots (our "Yes" to life) and our prophetic uprooting (our "No" to enemies of life such as injustice of all kinds). The key word in understanding spirit and prayer remains *life*. Dietrich Bonhoeffer, the Lutheran saint who was killed for opposing Hitler, wrote from his cell: "Jesus calls persons not to a new religion, but to life." And Erich

7. David Elkind, *The Child's Conception of Prayer,* in *From Cry to Word* (Belgium: Lumen Vitae Press, 1968), 51–64.

Fromm, in his powerful book on evil, *The Anatomy of Human Destructiveness*, warns us that "necrophilia grows when *biophilia* is stunted." This book on prayer as a radical response to life is about putting *biophilia* (love of life) first. "God is life" (Hildegard of Bingen and Thomas Aquinas both said this), and so our response to life constitutes our response to the Life-giver, the Source of Life. Aquinas says that the Creator is "the fountain of life" who renders us drunk, for "those who hold their desire at the fountain of life and sweetness are drunk."[8]

Leo Tolstoy is cited in this text (page 62) as saying "To know God and to live are the same thing: God is life." Or as Rabbi Abraham Joshua Heshel put it, "just to be is a blessing, just to live is holy."[9] To thank is to live life fully (page 86), and creativity derives its energy ultimately from gratitude. Meister Eckhart put it this way: "Becoming fruitful as a result of a gift is the only gratitude for the gift."[10] A passion and zest for life is what constitutes *biophilia* (cf. page 88 in this text). I am struck that if you put a one-inch band of steel around a young watermelon on a vine, it will break that steel as it grows. Isn't that *biophilia*? Are humans that much less in love with life than a watermelon? Can we share in its passion for living, its *biophilia*? Is that why the Christ says he has come to "bring life in abundance"?

Nor should the reader think that a life-affirming spirituality has dominated the history of western religion. Consider this passage from the hugely influential *Imitation of Christ* by Thomas a Kempis:

> The more violence you do to yourself, the greater will be your growth in grace. . . . There is no other way to life and

8. Fox, *Sheer Joy*, 110.
9. See Matthew Fox, *Original Blessing* (New York: Jeremy P. Tarcher, 2000), 42.
10. Matthew Fox, *Meditations with Meister Eckhart*, (Santa Fe: Bear & Co., 1982), 77.

> to true inward peace save the way of the holy cross, and
> of daily mortification. . . . Man must think of himself as
> he really is: nothing. . . . Truly to know and despise one-
> self is the best and most perfect counsel. . . . Every time
> I go into creation I withdraw from God.[11]

This spirituality is as self-focused as it is negative. The entire concern is God and self, self and God. The word "justice" is nowhere to be found in the entire book.

A second example of very influential fall/redemption thinking comes from the seventeenth-century French cardinal and preacher, Jacques Bénigne Bossuet. In the following sermon he speaks of human sexuality.

> Cursed by the earth, cursed be the earth, a thousand
> times cursed be the earth from which rises continually
> that heavy fog and those black vapors which ascend from
> these dark passions and hide heaven and its light from us
> and draw down the lightning and rays of divine justice
> against the corruption of the human race.[12]

This put-down of earth, our own earthiness, and sexuality is an affront to the Creator God.

Some thoughts expressed in this book still entice and challenge me, as I hope they will the reader. Among them are the following:

> The function of grace is not to do, but to behold.
> (page 63)

---

11. Thomas a Kempis, *The Imitation of Christ*, trans. A. Croft (Milwaukee: 1940), I, 25; II, 12; I, 24.
12. Jacques Bénigne Bossuet, *Traite de la concupiscence*.

Signs of the true prophet include a willingness to per-
sonlly reroot oneself and develop a mystical life; a reluctance for the prophetic role; creativity; community
orientation and commitment; and a willingness to pay
the price. (pages 109–116)

The prophet or spiritual warrior suffers the new life into
existence and whatever suffering accompanies the prophetic vocation is not self-induced but brought about by
angering outside powers-that-be. (page 114)

To be radical is to acknowledge that we are all in trouble.
(page 70)

Every adult has a prophetic vocation to speak out against
forces of death (necrophilia). (page 105)

Radical means spiritual. (page 109)

Hope is not optimism but the capacity to sustain one's
belief that life is a gift when all else seems to dictate otherwise. (page 115)

The psychological can never replace the social. (page 123)

Where life is sought for its own sake lies the spiritual
(page 153)—consider Eckhart, who urges us to "live without a why" and teaches that life "lives for its own sake."[13]

13. See Matthew Fox, *Passion for Creation: The Earth-Honoring Spirituality of
Meister Eckhart* [formerly *Breakthrough*] (Rochester, Vermont: Inner Traditions),
203–205

The tension between mysticism and prophecy is treated in depth in this book, and rightly so. "Adult prayer is nothing if it is not life lived on a level of mysticism and prophecy. And a life lived at a deepening level of mysticism and prophecy *is* a life of adult prayer." (page 153) How are we doing? How effective is our "radical responding to life"?

I cannot judge others on this matter, but I do know that the writing of this book has been pivotal to my own efforts at living a spiritual life. Without the concepts herein I would have folded my tent a long time ago and gone a more solitary route. I would not have been encouraged and even blessed to travel the path I have, a path that has been full of surprises and at times considerable pain. But it is one that has never grown dull or overly familiar. I am deeply blessed to have been able to live thirty years beyond the writing of this book and to have filled it out with twenty-some subsequent books, and to be able now to look back to how the living of it has fared. I claim no successes, nor do I judge an awful lot of my path as failure. I just keep going and notice that a lot of wonderful people—students and faculty, staff and coworkers, artists, activists, troublemakers, and wounded healers—have been crossing paths with me and I with them over these years. That we have been able to launch a University of Creation Spirituality, where people can study and deepen this tradition and create an impact to forge a renaissance for our time, is also a great blessing. As I write this preface, we are preparing to launch two new tracks in that University: one in "Creation Spirituality and the Indigenous Mind," and another in "Creation Spirituality and Sacred Cinema." Both are needed; both can help change our ways of being on this earth. For that I am immeasurably thankful.

The last word of this book belongs to musician Gustav Mahler. So, the final word of this preface belongs to Arthur Rubenstein.

I have noticed through experience and through my own observations that Providence, Nature, God, or what I would call the Power of Creation, seems to favor human beings who accept and love life unconditionally. And I am certainly one who does, with all my heart.[14]

May we all follow suit. Amen.

December 21, 2000 (my sixtieth birthday)
University of Creation Spirituality
Naropa Oakland
Oakland, California
www.creationspirituality.com

14. Arthur Rubenstein, *My Young Years* (New York: Popular Library, 1973), 488. Rubenstein's use of the term "unconditionally" in this passage and throughout his biography corresponds, it seems to me, exactly to my use in this book of the word "radical" (see chapter 3).

CHAPTER 1

What Prayer is Not

In pursuing a generic meaning for prayer it is first necessary to dismiss those popularized specific definitions of prayer with which catechism and uncritical texts have too long burdened us. It is not enough to leave the essence of religion, namely a meaning for prayer, un–thought out. Our quest is one of scientific research into the question of the meaning of prayer. To speak of a "definition" for prayer is dangerous, because prayer resides where easy categories and rational distinctions dare not enter, namely in man's prerational and nonrational experience. Nevertheless there are several kinds of definition and we seek a descriptive one. For to abandon altogether a search for a common understanding of prayer is to abandon the possibility of thinking about it together and even of communicating with one another about this reality, the very core of religion.

Those who caution us against relegating prayer to a definition are the patron saints of this chapter, for they argue our case for us; namely, that only a fundamental and generic description of prayer does prayer justice. Though the title of this chapter might sound negative and carping, in fact to distinguish one reality from another is a useful way of knowing, as any baby learning to distinguish his toes from his head and his arms from his mother's arms will witness to. Our method in this chapter, while it denies the status of a generic definition to many classical substitutes for prayer, investigates what is authentic in previous understandings of prayer and what can be applied to developing an American spirituality today.

The logic here is simple, though to some it may prove startling. A genus is not adequately contained in a species. A species does not exhaust, and therefore does not define fundamentally or generically, a genus. For example: "Sports is not baseball." Sports is not exhausted by baseball and to imply that it is is to deal with baseball as if it were a genus, i.e., the only sport; it is to rob one of swimming and tennis and surfing and horseback riding. At the same time, the proposition "sports is not baseball" does not signify that "baseball is not (or cannot be) a kind of sport."

1. PRAYER IS NOT SAYING PRAYERS

Pope-Hennessy's study on slave traders in America, *Sins of the Fathers*, reveals how respectable Englishman John Newton packed suffocating human beings chained to one another into the hold of his ship and then retired to his comfortable cabin to read the Bible and say his prayers. William Evarts composed a ditty on our pious Pilgrim ancestors: "The pious ones of Plymouth, reaching the Rock, first fell on their knees, and then upon the Aborigines."

But we do not have to look backward to our ancestors to appreciate how saying prayers is so easily confused with being a prayerful people—a simple confusion of the stuff passing for the substance or, in philosophical terms, the material of prayer being taken for prayer's formality. In 1958 in our country a study of the roles of the ministers during the Little Rock integration crisis revealed three classes of clergymen: those who pushed for integration; those who privately were for it but silent because their duty was to hold the church together; and those whose specialty was to pray for guidance, which is "how to say something without being heard."

Jesus scores the abuse of prayer in the name of saying prayers when he castigates the public religious officials of his religion: "Beware of the scribes . . . these are the men who swallow property of widows while making a show of lengthy prayers. The more severe will be the sentence they receive" (Mark 12:38–40). "And when you pray do not imitate the hypocrites; they love to say their prayers standing up in the synagogues and at the street corners for people to see them. I tell you solemnly, they have had their reward. In your prayers do not babble as the pagans do, for they think that by using many words they will make themselves heard. Do not be like them" (Matt. 6:5ff.).

Here Jesus puts his finger on the problem with identifying being prayerful with saying prayers: that of hypocrisy, the key sin for a believer. Hypocrisy can take place publicly (in the case of those standing up in the synagogues and on street corners) or privately, that is, within the heart and consciousness of individuals who believe they are pleasing God when in fact they are not (as in the case of the Pharisee's prayer in Luke 18:9–14). "Official" religious pray-ers—those whom society elevates as models of prayer—so often run the risk of the Pharisee.

For Jesus, the real concern of prayer is not saying prayers; it is the field or matrix in which prayers are said. In philosophical categories, it is not the formality of praying (saying) but the materiality or the setting for the prayer. Is it set in a context of justice and love of neighbor? Or is it as divorced from this setting as was the English slave trader who said his prayers, no doubt piously, on the very ship by which he made a living in the cargo of human beings. For Jesus a prayerful attitude is primary; that is, an attitude of love of neighbor and thereby of one's God, and the saying of prayers is presumed after that. He stops short those who identify prayer with saying of prayers: "Not all who say 'Lord, Lord' shall enter into the kingdom of heaven, but those who do the will of the Father" (Matt. 7:21). To do the will of his Father is to do the truth: to live out "justice, mercy, good faith."

Jesus demanded social obligations of justice before prayer. "So then, if you are bringing your offering to the altar and there remember that your brother has something against you, leave your offering there before the altar, go and be reconciled with your brother first, and then come back and present your offering" (Matt. 5:23–24). Thus, for Jesus, the social dimension of justice is a requisite for genuine prayer. He is saying that if people are too wrapped up in themselves or too psychologically sick to go out to others or too blind to see that justice is what one must make with others (i.e., that the given is injustice in the world), then prayer is no legitimate substitute for one's fears, timidity, and ignorance. On the contrary, to hide behind the skirts of prayer in such a non-just-making existence is to add hypocrisy to one's life of injustice. Prayer by whatever name takes no precedence over social justice.

The emphasis on justice and one's just moral setting for prayer is an emphasis in Matthew's Gospel, while the emphasis in Luke's Gospel (often called, inaccurately, the Gospel of Prayer) is on liturgical and cultic prayer. The reason for this difference in approaches to prayer is that Matthew's Gospel was intended for persons who already had some contact with prayer in their lives (those who were in need of a critique of their prayer), while Luke's was intended for newcomers to prayer (who could find exhilaration in Jewish worship). The approach in this book is also one to a Matthean audience; that is, for those who have at one time or another been taught either by their culture or by direct pedagogy something about prayer. For us, as for Matthew's audience, the key problem is bogus, hypocritical prayer.

In insisting that prayer is not saying prayers (cf. Tillich's distinction between praying and saying), we are not claiming that saying prayers might not be able to effect a prayerful people. Only that the saying of prayers is no longer, after Jesus' teaching, the constitutive factor of prayer. In fact it was not in the Jewish Old Testament prayer either. The profession of faith of the Israelite nation, the Shema, a daily recited prayer, was moral in its content: "Listen, Israel, Yahweh our God is the one Yahweh. You shall love Yahweh your God with all your heart." The nearest equivalent to our word for prayer among the Jews is the word "tefillah" which means a service of the heart: "you shall serve the Lord your God" (Exod. 23:25). While Jesus cannot be shown to have condemned nonspontaneous prayer (he himself prayed the daily prayers, including the Shema, the Hallel, and the Eighteen Benedictions as well as prayers at meals of his Judaic religious culture), the single prayer that he left for his disciples, the Our Father, far from being received in a formalized and fixed formula, has actually been handed on to us in two distinct versions, Matthew's and Luke's.

Jesus levels his abuse not only at the saying of prayers but also at the piety that so often accompanies it. His indictment of the scribes and Pharisees in Matthew spares no anger in pronouncing his judgment on the pseudopious: "Hypocrites," "blind guides," "fools," "whitewashed tombs," "lawless serpents," "brood of vipers," and finally "murderers." These are the epitaphs Jesus reserves for the pious; note, not for the prostitutes, nor for the thieves, nor for the sick and eyesore lepers, nor even for the wealthy, but for the pious. And why is he so unbending in this judgment? Because such pious strutting neglects "the weightier matters of the Law; justice, mercy, good faith!" They neglect to clean the inside of themselves which is full of extortion and intemperance. It is because saying prayers or performing other pious duties (paying tithes, building monuments to religion, obeying the Mosaic Law in its details and exaggerating these details, converting others) profits a man nothing when the basis and the matrix of prayer, namely love of neighbor, is lacking. "He who says he loves God [and, one can add, prays to him] and hates his neighbor is a liar" (1 John 4:20).

Jesus' attack on pharisaical piety indicates that he destroyed prayer as comfort. The descriptions of Jesus in prayer are not descriptions of a person in pietistic comfort complete with air-

conditioned breezes and velvet cushions. His prayers take place
amid groanings and sweatings of blood and shedding of tears
and wrestling with evil spirits—in his retreat to the desert, in
the Garden of Gethsemane before his death, on the cross of
death, at the tomb of his dead friend Lazarus. Far from being
comfortable, Jesus' prayer is accompanied by suffering or by
extreme joy or anxiety, as before his choice of apostles or before
his messianic baptism.

2. PRAYER IS NOT WITHDRAWAL FROM ONE'S CULTURE

Man on a spiritual quest seems continually tempted to withdraw to a more holy place. But the idea that to pray he must
stop his relationship to the world about him (whether "stop" is
taken as finding a refuge of silence or means to leave the world)
is not as sacrosanct in Christian history as superficial commen-
taries on Christian spirituality would have us believe. This is
shown not only because the sacramental spirituality developed
in the Middle Ages was based on a reverence for created things
—water for baptism, fire for the Paschal mystery, bread and
wine, oils, candles—but especially because a false myth exists up
to this day declaring that a medieval monk withdrew from his
culture. (This is especially significant for Catholic spirituality,
since the monk's life is such a paradigm psychologically and
socially for Catholic prayer). In fact, at the height of monasticism, monks were at the heart of political power (they furnished
numerous popes in an age when the pope was the ultimate
temporal ruler); of economic power (their farms were so large
and prosperous in an agriculturally based economic era that one
chronicler could state: "The Abbot is even richer than the
Bishop." Cluny monastery was so wealthy that to this day the
neighboring farmers resent all monastic communities, as the
founders of Taize learned); of educational power (where else
did youths go to school for centuries?); and also of artistic power

(yes, the monks did copy classical manuscripts for posterity to enjoy). When monasticism tumbled as a cultural power in the twelfth and thirteenth centuries, it was precisely because the market place was moving away from the land and into the cities. The economic and political foundations of western culture were giving way in the wake of movements from farms to cities, from provincial stability to international mobility, from land wealth to capitalism and money as wealth.

The prayer of Jesus, too, was not a matter of withdrawal from his culture. On the contrary, his ultimate act of sacrifice and teaching, his assassination, was carried out precisely because he insisted (against the "withdrawal" advice of his followers) on entering the capital city when the word was in the air that his life was in danger. And it was in danger precisely because he had stood up to the powers of his culture with the kind of abusive criticism we have seen already. The moments of prayerful withdrawal on Jesus' part, as when he went alone to a section of Gethsemane to face his forthcoming death, were moments in preparation for his fuller and more whole entry into struggle with the powers and principalities of his culture.

The prayer of Jesus as recorded in the New Testament is invariably linked with the struggle to accept his messianic vocation. His retreats to the desert, like his going apart from his disciples in the Gethsemane garden, were not options for an ultimate withdrawal so much as a preparation for his throwing himself totally into the cultural arena of religious debate and social polemic, a choice that cost him his life. From his retreats to the desert he returned to pick his disciples, to submit himself to John the Baptist's baptism, i.e., to carry out his messianic calling. Withdrawal of place, then, is meant as a means to becoming a deeper pray-er and should not be confused with the essence of prayer.

The principle involved here has unfortunately gone unrecognized in many organized attempts to develop prayerful persons, e.g., novitiates, seminaries, and the like, where withdrawal from one's own culture, instead of being an opportunity to more fully meditate on one's vocation to one's culture, has meant a total immersion into another culture, very often a Roman ecclesiastical one. The sad result is that prayerful withdrawal becomes an endurance test, and when the endurance period is ended one emerges with little or nothing profound to say to one's culture. I met a religious sister who, before she entered the convent, knew all there was to know about cultivating a field; but the test of her knowledge in the new culture imposed by the convent was whether she could dust in corners.

Quietism as a psychological withdrawal has been formally condemned by most every church thinker, but there has been, at least since the French Revolution, a quietism of a *social* kind whose consequences have been even more devastating than that of any neurotic withdrawn mystic. Even some of Christianity's biggest heroes were so withdrawn from the culture in which they lived that they missed the spiritual battles of that culture. Vincent de Paul, for example, for all he did on a personal basis for individuals, still prolonged the medieval hoax of defining "charity" on a one-to-one basis of almsgiving. It was left to nonchurch thinkers, Voltaire, for example, to grasp the justice dimension of social concern. The French Revolution followed, and since that turning point in contemporary self-consciousness, Catholic prayer and spirituality have been notable neither for their courage nor their greatness of vision but for their egocentricity. *God and Me* was the title of Newman's spiritual autobiography, and he was among the best of Catholic spirituals of the nineteenth century. Pietism reigned in much of Protestant spirituality so that to pray seldom meant to criticize one's cultural milieu. Pietism took the protest out of Protestant spirituality.

What is always lamentable in a private withdrawal, whether it be psychologically accomplished or institutionally brought about, is an attitude of considering prayer as personal or institutional calisthenics or spiritual muscle-building. "I may be preoccupied with my health, my fortune, or even with my inward perfection," warns Marcel. This subjectivization or privatization of prayer reduces the *Our* Father to a *My* Father. The privatization of Christian spirituality reduced God's providence and the grace of Jesus Christ to the "church" and to holding up private tête-à-têtes with God as an ultimate ideal, and thus defining prayer as "God talking with man" and vice versa. Meanwhile, the "world" (i.e., nonchurch) went its own way, oblivious of any Christian contribution to its nonprivate (i.e., its economic, social, and political) struggles. Church cultures, both Protestant and Catholic, became useless and powerless because they surrendered the only power they possessed: a spiritual power, or power to motivate and incite men to bigger visions than their culture possessed. These church cultures, eager to maintain their own existence, even allowed their privatized condition to dictate their definition of prayer and therefore the way they prayed. In America, religion stood against sexual promiscuity and against drinking but was silent on systematic castration of black human beings for two centuries as well as on the matter of war machinery and war-making.

For Catholicism, Vatican II marked a turning point in its spirituality as the "world" was acknowledged as a rightful place to encounter God. Thus was continued the struggle with the postmedieval world intiated by the Reformation. Prayer, which follows as a center point of the new spirituality, finds itself in the position William James observed is essential:

If it [prayer] be not effective . . . if the world is not a whit different for its having taken place; then prayer . . . is of course a feeling of what is illusory, and religion must on the whole be classed, not simply as containing elements of delusion—these undoubtedly everywhere exist —but as being rooted in delusion altogether, just as materialists and atheists have always said it was.[1]

1. William James, *The Varieties of Religious Experience* (New York: Mentor Press, 1958), p. 353.

We have seen above that the material setting for prayer is constitutive of it, at least since the teaching of Jesus. The revolution of man's consciousness (and his unconsciousness) initiated with the Copernican revolution and continuing with the French Revolution, the Enlightenment, the Marxian and Freudian critiques, and the industrial, the atomic, the Einsteinian, and the technological revolutions are not incidental to prayer. On the contrary, they form the matrix, the very field and stuff of prayer. Prayer takes place as a wrestling with the spiritual powers and principalities (where spiritual means deep, living, and real) of one's world, of one's culture. The real tension regarding prayer today is not communal versus personal but one of formal versus material. This because the material for prayer, namely western culture, has undergone and continues to undergo so total a transformation.

3. PRAYER IS NOT ACQUIESCENCE TO A CULTURE

It is one thing not to withdraw from a culture and call that withdrawal (which invariably becomes an option for another culture) a lofty spiritual act of prayer, and it is another to stay within a culture and accept all its values, especially its root ones, uncritically. Jesus did not withdraw from his culture. But he did thoroughly engage and attack its religious presuppositions, including its prayer. So significant is this point for our study on prayer that we must take up the question in some depth. It is best put in the following manner: Did Jesus destroy the prayer of Israel?

Jewish prayer was unique in comparison with its Egyptian and Mesopotamian neighbors insofar as it was based on a historical confidence in Yahweh, emanating from the saving works of Israelite history; it was a corporate prayer recalling how Yahweh dealt with his people as a people though it did allow for a wholeness and respect for the individual pray-er (Moses, Samuel, Amos with his flock, Isaiah). In form, Jewish prayer might consist of poetry, as in the Psalms, or prose which lists the deeds of Yahweh in saving the history of his people. Prayer was never limited to a cult place in Judaism as it was among the neighboring religions of the Near East, yet prayer was associated with institutional places. Ordinarily the pious Jew could be expected to pray at an altar, a sanctuary, or a shrine. Above all, the Temple of Jerusalem came to symbolize Jewish prayer and Jewish hopes. When hopes were low regarding the messiah, for example, a disenchantment with the Temple set in; when hopes were high the Temple was called a "house of prayer for all peoples" (Isa. 56:7).

The synagogue, a postexilic phenomenon corresponding to the diaspora or dispersion of the Jews, reinforced the Temple's symbolism at a local level in the absence of the Temple (the first synagogue is reported in Egypt in 230 B.C.). In the synagogue the cult was secondary; the emphasis was on preaching and instruction. There the Law and the prophets were listened to and the community engaged in common prayer.

In all ways Jesus was respectful of the prayer and piety of his ancestors. He uses the Psalms explicitly; he recites the Shema; he is faithful to the paschal tradition; he gives the usual blessing over food and drink; he visits the synagogue services; early Christians testify that he prayed morning, afternoon, and evening as do pious Jews (Didache 8:3); he prays in Aramaic; he wears the Jewish cloak. He carries on the spirit of Jewish prayer both in its moral imperatives for inward purity as we have seen and in its confidence in Yahweh who is now his "Father." "The Father will give you anything you ask him in my name" (John 15:16, cf. the parables of prodigal son; asking for fish versus snake, bread versus rock, etc.).

In Jesus' day Herod's work of restoring the Temple was almost completed. It had been a twenty-year job and the new building was no doubt a sparkling symbol of the Jewish cult. Jesus respects the Temple. He visits it on feast days, his first recorded words are from within it; he proclaims good news and works miracles of his messiahship within the Temple. The Gospel of Luke is actually built around the Temple, beginning with Simeon's prophecy within it and ending with the disciples continually in the Temple praising God. Jesus never says a word against the Temple, but calls it "my Father's house," "the house of God," a "house of prayer." Jesus purifies the Temple out of zeal for the house of his Father. His respect extends to the conduct he expects of others: "Nor would he allow anyone to carry anything through the Temple" (Mark 11:16).

Yet while Jesus does not attack the Temple directly he does undermine it; that is, he declares that the religious system of the Temple has come to an end and that the holiness of which the Temple was a symbol is achieved in a new cult. "As he was leaving the Temple one of his disciples said to him, 'Look at the size of those stones, Master! Look at the size of those buildings!' Jesus said to him, 'You see these great buildings? Not a single stone will be left on another: everything will be destroyed'" (Mark 13:1-2).

For the synoptics, the Temple is a place where man meets God; for John, it is a place where God dwells. For Jesus, acting as Messiah, it is himself. Ezekiel foretold a "new temple" would accompany the messianic era and Jesus says: "Destroy this temple and I will rebuild it in three days" (John 2:19). And, "Now here, I tell you, is something greater than the Temple. And if you had understood the meaning of the words, 'What I want is mercy, not sacrifice,' you would not have condemned the blameless. For the Son of man is master of the sabbath" (Matt. 12:6-8).

Jesus is saying that the true sanctuary is his body, which will be baptized by the fire and baptism of his own bloody death. "I have come to bring fire to the earth, and how I wish it were blazing already! There is a baptism I must still receive, and how great is my distress till it is over" (Luke 12:49-50). When he suffers and dies the veil will rip open in the Temple, a sign of the new sanctuary that replaces all other kinds of worship. Now he is the vine, not Israel; he is the cornerstone of the new worship that he has proclaimed and that is an "eschatological replacement of temporal institutions like the Temple."[2] "But the hour will come—in fact, it is here already—when true worshipers will worship the Father in spirit and truth: that is the kind of worshiper the Father wants. God is spirit, and those who worship must worship in spirit and truth" (John 4:21–24).

In answer to our original inquiry, we can say that Jesus did destroy the prayer of his culture (a great scandal it was, for this was the prayer of the chosen race), but he did it by an in-depth replacement of that cult; he offered an alternative and not just a critique of that prayer. He was respectful though forceful and thorough in his replacement. Is not Jesus' replacement of the Temple the reason for his trial and death? (A strong case could be made for this argument.)

The early Christians followed their Lord in his rejection of their culture's prayer. First of all, and most startlingly, baptized Christians believed that they themselves were a new Temple; they appropriated Jesus' assertion that he replaced the Temple to those who had been reborn in baptism in this same Jesus (1 Cor. 3:16–17). Their persecution as atheists is directly related to their refusal to worship as their Roman culture dictated, and when they did acquiesce, only after three centuries, to building their own churches and buildings and thereby paralleling Roman worship, the persecutions ceased. At this point in Christian history, with Constantine's conversion and the edict of Milan allowing the Christians to inherit the Roman cultural empire, official and cultic prayer among Christians took on a parallel value with honoring the state and culture. To pray was a sign of a good citizen from then until the French Revolution. It was also at this point that Christian protest commenced and anchoritism, the retreat to the desert to wrestle with spiritual de-

2. Raymond Brown, *The Gospel According to John i-xiii* (New York: Doubleday & Co., 1966), p. 180.

mons, spread so suddenly. "It was not by chance that anchoritism, the retreat to the desert, spread so suddenly just as the
State made its peace with the Church."[3] In the seventeenth
century, the hermits of Port Royale withdrew from their culture. Far from seeking a spiritual isolation, they were protesting
the alignment of church and French principalities under the
aegis of Cardinal Richelieu. One senses that the current
eremetical interest in America also derives from a spirit of protest to one's cultural priorities.

4. PRAYER IS NOT CAUSING GOD TO CHANGE BY OUR PETITIONS

Huckleberry Finn was reported to have prayed for a fishing
pole and hooks. But when he got only the pole, he gave up
prayer. In the psychological study on prayer previously referred to, one conclusion reached was that "among the younger
children the content of prayer was concerned primarily with
gratification of personal desires." Thus Jimmy, aged seven and
a half, is asked, "What is prayer?" He replies, "That we should
have water, food, rain, and snow. It's something you ask God
for, water, food, rain, and snow."

A child lives in a world of petition: "I want, I need, I desire,
you give" are at the heart of his existence. Indeed, a child by
definition is a dependent person. Cause and effect to a child are
in terms of request and answer. But the child's world is not his
for long; he soon grows out of depending on others and accepts
his own capacity to affect his world. The child's prayer of petition cannot be the foundation of adult prayer.

Jewish prayer in the Old and New Testaments is not
primarily asking God for something. Prayer for the Jews, we
will recall, was primarily a thanking and recalling of the pres-

3. Louis Bouyer, *The Spirituality of the New Testament and the Fathers*
(London: Burns and Oates, 1960), p. 305.

ence of Yahweh in his people's history and among them personally. Yahweh cares and provides for his people and prayer is the
praise for Yahweh's concern. This constant, loving presence
Jesus reemphasized by underlining the intimacy characterizing
the presence of the Father. "My Father and I will dwell in you
and make our abode in you." "The Kingdom of God is within
you." Every hair on our head is numbered. The Father of the
Prodigal Son was waiting all the while.

An adult relationship with such a Father differs vastly from
a God on which a pray-er can bring about effect by registering
a prayer. The Father of whom Jesus speaks is a loving Father
and friend. But a friend is not one whom we ask to do things
for us so much as one who is with us. By his or her presence we
are supported and encouraged in doing what we must do. A
friend is one who allows us to change simply by being with us.
And so it was in the prayer of Jesus. In Gethsemane he first
begged that the chalice of his awful death be removed; but such
was not the will of his Father. So the result of his prayer was
Jesus' being changed, to accept and undergo the chalice he so
dreaded. Prayer is man being changed, not God. Kierkegaard
says, "Prayer does not change God, but it changes the one that
offers it." And Thomas Aquinas follows suit: "By prayer man
renders himself capable of receiving" *(Comp. theol.,* II, c.2).

Prayer of petition dominates not only the minds of children
but also the minds of prescientific cultures. Science by definition is man's discovery of the causes and effects of his world:
Providence is not needed as a part of the equations of natural
science. The predominance of science in the western mentality
since the Copernican revolution has gradually relegated prayer
as petition to a status of superstition. The attempt by rational
philosophers to find a place and a job for the God emeritus of
western culture only succeeded to reduce Providence to a
cause (one gets the impression from Newton that were God not
busy oiling the universe he would have nothing constructive to
occupy his time), and prayer than becomes a tripping of the

Great Cause in the Sky into action. The God of the Jews remains, but neither as lord of a technological culture nor as a captive of cause and effect. He refuses to be moved from his relationship, which is one of a loving, creative presence. Religion unattuned to science will make prayer synonymous with petition. A negative spirituality emphasizing man's limitation, his lack of self-realization and affirmation, will attribute all secondary causes to God (fundamentalist sects, anti-intellectual at their base, flourish on this). But a humanist spirituality, one that accepts man as God's image in the universe, joins chorus with science's respect for the unlimited capacity of man to know and affect the universe. Aquinas, for example, who in humanist fashion felt that one human mind can know potentially all things, understood awe or adoration, not petition, as the touchstone to prayer.

The adult question to put to prayer is: Who is asking what of whom? There is ample evidence in the Gospels as well as in the magnanimous deeds of believers from Abraham to today to suggest that it is not we who ask for God's action in prayer but it is he who waits for us to become what we already are; to act with a new Spirit and a new vision with the new worship through his son who made "all things new" and prays that the same may be accomplished through us (John. 17).

Prayer in the Gospels is not magic; it is not a commercial bartering, a tit for a tat. It is a loving presence responded to maturely. What petition is present (as in the Our Father) is found in the context of prayer of praise (the Our Father's first three petitions) and thanks, and its keynote is confidence in the Father's loving interest and love, not in the request one's tiny heart or puny theory of Providence may have devised.

5. PRAYER IS NOT TALKING TO GOD

The psychological study on prayer referred to earlier reveals that nine-to twelve-year-olds understood prayer as a conversation with God. Yet how many adults have yet to outgrow the preadolescent definition of prayer as "talking with God"?

The Gospels do not support an understanding of prayer as primarily talking with God. If prayer means talking with God, then what sense do the "pray always" themes of the New Testament make? Jesus was said to be "praying always" (Luke. 18:1, cf. Eph. 5:18–20); but how is this so when he drove moneychangers from the Temple, or when he conversed with the Temple teachers as a young man? In what sense was he, throughout his life, "praying always" if this means conversing with God? Paul, too, teaches the early Christians of Thessalonica (1 Thess. 5:17; cf. 2 Thess. 1:3, 1:11, 2:13) to "pray at all times"; but how was Paul constantly "talking with God" when he was swimming for his life after the shipwreck at Malta? Or when he was racking his brain for eloquent testimony in the public square at Athens? Men who have reflected on Christian prayer through history concur when they say life is "one great continuous prayer" (Origen), or "there is an interior prayer without ceasing" (Augustine), or "men of religious genius remain in continuous contact with God through prayer" (Heiler), or "we cannot hold conversation with God" (Von Balthasar), or the Reformation itself was "an act of continuous prayer" (Barth). We can only conclude that prayer's primary meaning cannot be conversation with God but concerns the presence, the medium, the field of prayer where we "live, move and have our being" (Acts 17:28) in a God who is "over all, works through all, and is in all," a "being rooted and grounded in love" (Eph. 3:17) who is God. Moments of prayer labelled "talking with God" are either derived from this primary field for Christian prayer or they are not prayer at all.

With the scientific revolution inaugurated with Copernicus, philosophers such as Descartes tried to defend faith by constructing our knowledge processes on a concept of subject-object relationships. God, who was clearly not subject, was taken to be the object of one's petitions and one's conversation.

But God is not conceivable as an object of our prayer, and such a situation leads directly to atheism, as both Marcel and Tillich suggest. "We can only pray to the God who prays to himself through us. Prayer is a possibility only insofar as the subject-object structure is overcome."[4]

More recently, Martin Buber (in *I and Thou*), and personalist philosophers after him, emphasize that God is not an object in any sense of the word, but a personal "thou" with whom one communicates. Thus they have broken once and for all the objectivization of God that had saddled prayer for at least three centuries. But this notion of prayer also has its intrinsic limitations. First of all, in what sense is God a person? One must say that primarily (and we are concerned in this study with primary meanings since the secondary in the question of prayer have held sway for too long) God is *not* a person—analogy tells us more what a thing is not than what it is—God lies beyond all experience of ours of person and personality. The "persona" of the Trinity used to distinguish Father, Son, and Spirit is just that: a conceptual device to distinguish Father, Son and Spirit; it is not meant to be confused with our making God over into an image of person in the rich though anthropomorphic understanding that modern personalism has provided it with. God is analogously a person and thus we learn something about him (or better, we unlearn more ignorance about him) by applying such a category as person to him analogously. But primarily he is not a person. "The God to whom one prays is said to be a person. The difficulty is that this suggests an idea of God as a finite individual. There is so much of what can be said about God which makes this suggestion absurd, that one wonders why it is made at all."[5]

God is primarily God. "God," insists Marcel, "is not 'Someone

4. Paul Tillich, *Systematics*, III, 119f.
5. D. Z. Phillips, *The Concept of Prayer* (New York: Schocken Books, 1966), p. 43.

Who.' . . . The more non-disposable I am, the more will God appear to me as 'Someone Who.' . . . This lays bare the very roots of atheism. The God who atheism denies is in fact a 'Someone Who' in his very essence."[6]

To say prayer is our talking to God is to risk reducing prayer to talking to ourselves. The brunt of the concept of prayer as "talking to God" falls on one's understanding of language and talking. The question at hand is well put by Phillips: "Is God a participant in language?" If so, then to know how to use that language is to know God. The God-language Jews and Christians believe in is called Revelation. "At various times in the past and in various different ways, God spoke to our ancestors through the prophets; but in our own time, the last days, he has spoken to us through his Son" (Heb. 1:1–2). Thus Jesus Christ is in a literal sense the Word (*logos*) of the Father, spoken definitively to mankind. God's word to mankind is a human person. To know him is to know the Father. "No one has ever seen God; it is the only Son, who is nearest to the Father's heart, who has made him known" (John 1:18). How often one hears, "I prayed for hours and received no word or answer from God," when the word "pray" has come to mean one expects a whispering in one's ear or consciousness. All along God has put his Word in the midst of man's historical and personal life, and this Word by his example and his grace does communicate with man. If only we were attuned to God's language which is spoken in the flesh. "Philip, have I been with you all this time and you do not know me?" (John. 14:9).

The commonly held assumption that prayer is dialogue with God has held sway for so long that it might be helpful to examine the origin of such a definition. It is to superficial and misinterpretations of the Greek fathers that we owe this misunderstanding of prayer. Origen, in his *Peri Euches* (231–34), presents the oldest discussion extant dedicated exclusively to Christian

6. *Being and Having* (New York: Harper & Row, 1965), p. 81.

prayer, and in it he concludes that "the whole life of the saint is one great continuous prayer" (xii. 2.47). Clement of Alexandria describes the ideal of the perfect man in communion with God and he defines prayer as the "uninterrupted converse *(homilia)* with God by knowledge, life and thanksgiving" *(Stromateis,* vii. 7). Aside from the conspicuous absence of the notion of prayer as petition in these definitions, what is the fuller meaning behind them?

Origen (ix. 2), Gregory *(Homilies,* i. 1124D), and Clement employ the Greek word *homilia* or its root verb *homilein* for prayer. The meanings possible to this word are the following: 1) to be together or in company with, to associate with; 2) to come or live together; 3) to meet in battle, encounter; 4) to hold converse; to live familiarly with, associate with; to have dealings with; 5) to be friends. Thus the translation we have received of *homilein* as "talking" is simply inaccurate. A second word sometimes employed by the Greek fathers for prayer is *dialexis* (from which we get the English "dialect"), which can mean discourse, conversation, debate, argument, speech, language, or dialect. Again, this word is not properly translated as "talking" or "speaking." Rather, its use for prayer raises our fundamental question in this book; namely, what shall the proper language (dialect) be between man and God? How shall we discourse with God?[7]

6. PRAYER IS NOT LITURGY

The liturgist does not consider the nature of prayer but presumes that prayer is actually happening in liturgies. To the extent that liturgy never asks whether man is praying or need pray at all, to that extent the discussion of prayer in this book is not about liturgy at all. This is not to say that our treatment of prayer does not hold implications for worship, however, for

7. Robert L. Simpson, *The Interpretation of Prayer in the Early Church* (Philadelphia: The Westminster Press, 1965), pp. 33f., 153.

the more and more evident fact to those who are in dialogue with persons in search of prayer is that so often they not only do not find it in liturgy but are repelled by the liturgy. To mention just one example: I met a man in his middle twenties who came to me saying that the liturgy was so stilted, the preaching so unrelated to the very busy life he was living in the capital city he was in, and the relationship set up between priest and congregation so formalized that every time he attended Mass he returned home angry. Since his purpose in prayer was not to get himself worked up to a point of anger, his decision was not to attend liturgy anymore. Judging from the diminishing numbers attending liturgical services in our country (especially missing are the youth, many of whom seek prayerful lives), it would seem that this is by no means an isolated example of the gap between liturgy and prayer.

This gap is a serious matter; not because filling churches is a "command of God," but because it hints of the dread reality of the corruption of prayer. The judgment on liturgy made by this young man and more like him (so many of whom could hardly be more sincere and eager for prayer) is a judgment that liturgy is in serious danger of becoming magic and hollow ritual.

The high point of prayer for the Jews of the Old Testament is decidedly not during the period of stabilization of prayer according to the law and the liturgy that occurred during the last five centuries before Christ, and was a relatively late development in the Jews' relationship to Yahweh. In fact, the high point of the Jews' intimacy with Yahweh was considered to be the period of the desert wanderings (Amos 5:25; Hos. 9:10; Jer. 2:2). This period was a nomadic one for the Jews and provided little opportunity for elaborate liturgies.

The reason liturgy does not suffice as a primary understanding of Christian prayer is that "we have not been redeemed by an act of pure worship, a liturgical service."[8] Calvary was not

8. Edward Schillebeeckx, *God the Future of Man* (New York: Sheed and Ward, 1968), p. 99.

a church liturgy; in fact, its prayer took place outside all sacred precincts, even outside the holy city of Jerusalem. Yet we have made the reenactment of Calvary and the Last Supper to be almost exclusively liturgical.

Taking these factors into consideration, who can overestimate the damage by silence wrecked on the people of God and those who would like to have worked with them through the centuries by a suffocating reduction of the Christian priest to a performer of rituals? It is relatively efficient to train, to classify, and to pay priests by their altar status, but the price one pays for this is expensive psychologically and socially as events of the past centuries indicate. For in principle (if not yet in fact), "the priesthood is essentially a prophetic rather than simply a ritual priesthood."[9] Taking this belief seriously was the inspiration that led Camilo Torres, living in a seemingly incurable state of human injustice, to quit his liturgical vocation "temporarily," as he put it, to first devote himself to reconciliation: "I have stopped offering Mass to live out the love for my neighbor in the temporal, economic, and social order. When my neighbor no longer has anything against me . . . then I will offer Mass again, if God so wills it. I believe that in this way I am following Christ's injunction."[10] I was once a participant in a three-day international convention of utmost importance regarding issues of pressing social concern. When the heat got high and conflict and anger were on the floor openly, a delegation from the convention retreated from it, invoking the excuse of a liturgy. Anger meant it was liturgy time.

In saying prayer is not primarily liturgy, we are not saying that the Eucharist has no prayerful role to play, only that our inquiry here, which is a fundamental one of determining what a prayerful role might mean at all in today's culture, cannot be

9. Yves Congar, *Tradition and Traditions* (New York: Macmillan Co., 1967), p. 432.
10. Letter dated August 3, 1965.

satisfied with remaining silent about the basic questions of prayer that liturgy presumes. It is possible to pray without the liturgy, but there is no guarantee that one's presence at liturgy is thereby a prayerful presence.

The chasm between the noble theology of the liturgy, what it is supposed to be and do, and what it actually does in many people's experience is a gap between one culture and another totally different and emerging one. The fact is that for a growing number of persons, liturgy is rarely a prayer. The experience of liturgy as prayer (as opposed to liturgy as cult) will only be regained by a critical look at prayer. The initial experience of the liturgy as passage from the old to the new, from this world into the world to come, as procession and ascension to the Kingdom, "was obscured and replaced by its understanding in terms of a cult (public *and* private) whose main aim is to satisfy our religious needs. The *leitourgia*—a corporate procession and passage of the Church towards her fulfillment, the sacrament of the Kingdom of God—was thus reduced to cultic dimensions and categories among which those of obligation, efficiency, and validity acquired a central, if not exclusive position."[11]

7. PRAYER IS NOT AN EXCEPTIONAL EXPERIENCE.

It will be clear by now that the primary meaning of prayer that we are searching out in this book is not a moment here or there. No less is it an experience here or there. We are all familiar with the admonitions of Catholicism's "ideals" of prayer, such as John of the Cross and Teresa of Avila, who disclaim the importance of experiences in prayer. It is not the experience, they underline, that is significant. On whether one should even allow himself to enjoy mystical experiences John

11. Alexander Schmemann, "Prayer, Liturgy and Renewal." *Theology of Renewal*, II (New York: Herder and Herder, 1968), p. 83.

and Teresa disagree; the former, representing the negative
spirituality he inherited from the mystics of the low countries,
denies that one should actually enjoy himself in prayer, while
Teresa sees no problem in this pleasure. Both, however, insist
that the experience is not of the essence for prayer. Indeed, the
recent and weird prejudice that mysticism need be a special
grace of extraordinary phenomenon is not at all present in
ancient spiritual literature. Saint Bernard, writing for medieval
monks, recognizes two kinds of mystics: those who flourish in
apostolic works and those who do not (nothing said of trances).
Father Congrave has put the matter straight:

I do not think that a lover of God strains after any special sensible
consciousness of finding God, as if without some special reply . . . he
was forsaken . . . unable to go forward. The special charism of the saint
is that he *waits for nothing* (sic), for he *is in the way* (sic), being in
Christ—not a mere track, but a living way into the Holiest. . . . He does
not think it necessary that he should feel God . . . he knows that "in
Him we live and move and have our being." That is enough certainty
to travel by.[12]

To build a theology of prayer on mystical experience would
be like building a science of baseball on a no-hitter or a grand
slam home run, with the same consequences of discouraging
players to approach the game. One must ask if a mystic is very
often a saint in spite of, not because of, his or her mystical
experience. This would seem to be the case from reading com-
plaints of honest persons like Teresa of Avila.

Jesus, who left a cup in his memory that "all sins might be
forgiven," did not intend that prayer would be restricted to the
mystics (any more than that mystics should be excluded from it).
Prayer is a far simpler, a far more common and a far less distant
reality than many have been led to believe. The great pray-ers
of the past became such by their own experience with vision
and hope, despair and frustration, struggle and rejection with

12. *Spiritual Letters*, p. 81.

society, not by spending hours (or conjuring up feelings of guilt for not spending hours) panting after the prayer of others. In thinking on prayer and ourselves, the only unpardonable mistake will be our thinking we are not praying. This is unpardonable because it abrogates to ourselves what is truly the work of the Spirit.

An enforced tactical mysticism has for so long been a pattern in religious circles that it is worth pausing to examine. One can read, for example, of the "good old woman" who tells her beads "on a winter evening, in the chimney corner," and how these "tactics" are "a first stage, a humble beginning, on the path of mystical union."[13] The same author goes on to explain in his condescending way that this is "the only stage which most people are capable of reaching," yet he insists on continuing this mystical exercise, confident that nothing will come of it. This grotesque display of spiritual imperialism betrays the kind of paternalism that mysticism, so often constructed on a view of life and politics as hierarchical, is so often heir to. It plays into the hands of those who dismiss all mysticism as corrupt (cf. Feuerbach and the later Marx; for a discussion on nontactical or natural mysticism, see Chapter 4). Is it mere coincidence that the shrillest cries for tactical mysticism still emanate from the ex-nobles of Europe who long for reinstatement in their lost privileged places near the top of society's pyramid?

So much of prayer, like so much else in western civilization, has taken on that aura of competition and priggishness that Santayana detects in Aristotle's concepts of contemplation. The comfort and the rites so enjoyed by the aristocracy (whether royal or monastic, professionally religious or a monied aristocracy) becomes the norm for others' prayer, which is another way of keeping the nigger down, the nigger defined as all who pray differently from "us" (meaning our class).

13. Joseph Marechal, *Studies in the Psychology of Mystics*, trans. Algar Thorold (New York: Magi Books, 1964), pp. 157f.

"The corruption of the best is the worst" goes the old saying; and prayer, used as a weapon and a panacea in so many battles, has suffered such a corruption. This is particularly the case in America, where the subject of prayer so often receives devout nods of piety. It's amazing—the evil spirits that can hide behind the long skirts of piety! FBI directors expound on prayer; politicians invoke it and pretend to come to its defense in so-called school prayer bills; evangelists earn a good living on it. A good rule of thumb might be that those who so incessantly invoke it do so in inverse proportion to what they know of it. "Prayer, rather than science or reason," warns one critic of American society, "is the tool of the political medicine man."[14]

In reality, prayer is useless. To rediscover the useless yet valuable in life is to recover prayer. Those who try to make use of prayer do not respect prayer at all but manipulate it. Prayer is not a means but a value in itself. "It is not permitted to see in prayer a good work to do, a good pious thing, nice and beautiful. Prayer cannot be for us a means of creating something, of making a gift to God and ourselves."[15] Amen.

14. Ferdinand Lundberg, *The Rich and the Super-Rich* (New York: Bantam Books, 1969), p. 934.
15. Karl Barth, *Prayer* (Philadelphia: Westminster Press, 1946), p. 27.

CHAPTER 2

Life and Its Mysteries:
The Stuff of Prayer

Having exposed in the previous chapter the commonly held notions of prayer for their inadequacy, we can now begin our own positive construction of a meaningful understanding of prayer. We suggest in this chapter that the matrix, the material, the stuff for prayer is life itself. "Life is so beautiful, so light, so short, and a representation of it is always so ugly, so heavy and so long," warns Tolstoy. The philosopher might understand life as existence, the classical theologian as creation; I prefer, for theological as well as personal reasons, to understand life as life: "what you do while you're waiting to die," as Zorba the Greek would tell us.

Western civilization has so long been content with defining the spiritual in a Greek sense of the immaterial, the non-material, that even those claiming a heritage of the Hebrew faith have forsaken the Jewish understanding of spirit as life. For the Jew, spirituality meant first of all one's attitude, one's response to life. For the Jew of the Old Testament as well as the New (cf. Rev. 21:5–8), the word for life is in fact the word for spirit or principle of life. Three words can mean spirit in the Jewish language: *nefas*, signifying a vital spirit; *ruah*, which originally meant air in motion, or breath, and later took on the meaning of breath of life or wind (being translated in Greek as *pneuma* and in Latin as *spiritus*); and *nesamah*, meaning breath and translated in Greek as *pnoe* or *pneuma*. Simple observation convinced the Jew that breath is a principle of life, for one is alive if he has breath, dead when breath ceases. Life becomes the word for spirit.

IS "LIFE" TOO VAGUE?

If the matrix for the spiritual is to be grasped not as the nonmaterial (so that a flight from the everyday and the material is a supreme spiritual act) but as life-oriented, are we indulging in substituting one abstract notion for another? Life, of course, is not a mere concept but an experience. To face the objection that "life" is too vague I asked a group of eighth-graders (thirteen- to sixteen-year-olds) in a low-income, multiracial neighborhood in Chicago to express their understanding of life. Their unedited responses follow:

Life is being with people who you could call friends and friends are people you can trust and depend on if couldn't trust people and no people you could call your friends life would be like not living, you would be better off dead.

To me, life is music, baseball, science and God. That's *my* life. I like music so I play it. I like baseball so' I play it. I like science so I study it.

I think life is fun. I think life is a big party and you have to enjoy it while you can because some day you'll have to leave the party. I plan on having a lot of fun before I go even if the time comes tonight I'll be having lots of fun.

Some people have terrible life. Like they are not loved by anybody. They are bad and do all stupid things, when they are small. But when they are big, they never get jobs or good for nothing but bad name called. Then you go through a terrible life and sufferings.

Life is seeing the birds and flowers come up every spring. Life is colorful, without color the whole world looks dead, like one color makes it dole.

I'm not afraid of death. As far as I can see it there aren't too many things to live for today. I'm not saying I would kill myself but I'm not afraid to go out at night alone. There are good things about life that I like. For instance I like the summer cause I can walk around in shorts or put on my bikini and go to the beach and flirt around.

Try hard you will see some day that life is. If you start thinking about it now it will be hard, but if you do not start now, later on as you grow older it will be too late. Some people who are in narcotics they do not realize what they are doing to their lives. Later, maybe, they will find out but it will be too late. Life is so short you can hardly realize it as it goes.

These insights by adolescents on life not only dismiss the objection that "life" is vague but they judge those adults for whom life has lost its meaning, its power to excite. Is there something about our adulthood that saps our capacities to respond to life as a mystery, as a gift? Is there something about our adulthood that crushes the spirit?

MYSTERY VERSUS PROBLEM

The French philosopher and art critic Gabriel Marcel suggests that we postindustrial adults become so programmed to solving problems that we lose our capacity to wonder and become ecstatic at mysteries. A problem (from the Greek *proballo*, meaning to throw in front of) is an object. Like a tree fallen across a road it is outside of me, an obstruction, and may be resolved by removal or rearrangement. "A problem is something met with which bars my passage. It is before me in its entirety." A mystery, on the other hand, is something in which I find myself caught up and whose essence is therefore not to be before me in its entirety. A mystery is decidedly *not* an unsolvable problem that needs rearrangement or removal to be resolved. Marcel warns that we are engaged in a "fundamentally vicious proceeding" when we, whether as individuals or as a culture, "reduce a mystery to a problem."[1] Those who are

1. *Mystery of Being,* I (Chicago: Regnery Co., 1960), p. 260.

subject to this temptation are victims, he claims, of a "kind of corruption of the intelligence."

Mystery is not the solvable or the manageable. It is that which stops us short: which touches a need deeply felt in us: which changes us by attracting us outside of our own petty worlds that we carry around in our heads and that our culture carries around in its voice boxes (magazines, newspapers, television) to call to mind something bigger than ourselves, bigger than our daily problems. A mystery is something bigger than ourselves that calls us outside of ourselves; yet its presence is no less real within us than outside us. It becomes one with us by the very act of its presence to us. Mystery carries an imperative with it: if only that we *take the time* (is there any commodity worth more to contemporary man?) to consider it.

The experience of mystery, like so much of the imaginative side of our lives, has been cut off from modern experience and subject to a reductionism since the philosophies of the rational age of the eighteenth century. Under the impact of rationalism, mystery came to be defined as "the unknowable" so that, for example, the universe is a mystery only because we cannot at this time know it. The other side of Mars is a "mystery" to us today but when man arrives there in a few years it will no longer be a mystery. The implication of this understanding is, of course, that mystery is only temporary in human life; that it is dispensable like garbage is, and only needs to be eliminated by the ever-advancing marches of scientific discovery and method. This approach to mystery ignores the experience and testimony of numerous scientists, who in the pursuit of their vocation actually witness more of mystery in the unraveling of the historical and chemical genesis of reality; it harbors an initial bias: that man's greatest contributions are conscious acts of a clear and distinct intelligence.

Mystery is not merely the unknowable, the lacuna in our scientific store; mystery is more a plenitude, a cup running over in our midst. A child is often recognizable for his openness to mystery. For a child, all is mystery; his initial response to just about everything is to probe it, to ask questions of it, and in this sense an adult has much to learn (or relearn) about awe from a child. For the adult, some things present themselves as problems to be dealt with; others are mysteries to be appreciated or responded to as a child. An immature adult is notable for his constant running from mysteries (we call these people "shallow"), or for his constant running from problems (the religious fanatic is a prime example here; he labels all life a "mystery" and will be found in church hours on end instead of at home or work doing what needs and can be done for his family). Adult life is a life aware of the mysterious dimension to it: life as a life with mysteries, not only a life with its problems.

MYSTERIES IN OUR LIVES

If mystery is not able to be reduced to a problem or to a missing link in our store of knowledge, then it must somehow be identifiable in our experience. I would like to present a list of mysteries that I think most of us share in our experience; it is by no means an exhaustive list, but examples for reflection. You might profit from pausing here and making up your own list of mysteries of life and then comparing it with those I suggest.

1. Life, the primordial mystery. The first and most universal experience of mystery is the mystery of life itself, that which no one can deny or run away from, the mystery all share even if reluctantly as on a battlefield when the purpose is to extinguish the possibility for mystery in another, i.e., to rid him of his life. Even to talk of life is itself mysterious; we can only offer examples of our experiences that others may or may not have had. Pasternak has pointed out how delicately one must treat life when he insists that "life is never a material, a substance to be molded . . . it is infinitely beyond your or my obtuse theories about it."

Life is that which happens to us between our birth and our

death, beginning with the slap on the behind from the doctor
to the obituary in the paper that our funeral will be at a certain
time and place. To whom do we go to "know life"? So often it
is the less educated, formally speaking, who have something
worthwhile to say about the mystery of life. For life is first of all
survival and the poorer are the experts at survival. So much of
their time (life's sole quantitative measurement) is spent in survival that they readily become experts. They are the ones with
"savoir faire" (or "wisdom" in its Old Testament meaning) in
the original meaning of the phrase of "knowing how to make
it" when "making it" does not refer to test tube–making of life
but to surviving in life.

It is the one struggling to survive who teaches the primordial
mystery of life: the value of life itself. Thus looking at a newborn
baby (especially if it be one's own, particularly one's first, and
most especially if we are observing its very birth) is so often an
experience of mystery and of wonder at something greater than
ourselves. Not only the projections of our dreams for this bundle
of possibilities, but the very fact of its living at all (when nonlife
is so near temporally and physically to it) arouses the mystery
in us. Ask the mother who is close to her baby of life's intrinsic
value. But ask by observing her care and concern, not by direct
(and therefore problem-oriented) questions. To observe those
adults who are just barely making it—the poor or the drunk or
the prostitute (in her low-income position, not the new class of
hired-outs that an opulent society provides for) or the sick—is
to reexperience the tenuousness of life and the intrinsic value
of living. These are the people who will not let go of life. They
will fight for it to the end. Simply because it is there; because
it is theirs. The value of life is not polluted for them (and dis-
tracted for observers) by the "values" of the things they possess,
whether by deeds or degree or domain or reputation. Theirs is
a naked and wide-open struggle for all to observe: for their daily
bread; for a roof from the rain and excessive sun (palm branches
will do for that); for heat in cold winters; for some human com-

munication (here wine or beer or something better helps a great deal); in short, for survival. Survival is their problem. But life, the reason for their toil, is their mystery. It is not to be confused with moralities pronouncing "good" or "bad" on their actions or their styles of life (for moralities are for others to feel justified by and that is a stage of life beyond survival). Mystery simply is. As life is. And these people feel called in their own way to live out that mystery and to survive at all costs.

So often middle-class man and woman lose the sense of life as survival and therefore the mystery to which the survival problem points: life as a value to which one must say either Yes or No. The suburban "mad housewife" can so often be caught in the web of pseudosurvival problems (invariably linked with judgments, i.e., multiplied moralities pronounced by her neighbors or her husband's office-watchers) that all sense of mystery and worth seeps from her and her husband's life. Life is reduced to cleanliness and comparisons ("keeping up with the Joneses" and "keeping in" with the styles). Life itself becomes a problem. A thing to be solved. A new appliance to save for. A new promotion to be prepared and plotted for. Life goes on, but it is fully defined and circumscribed by the next problem to be solved. Mystery—the appreciation of life for its own sake—is excluded from the daily routine and gradually from the possibilities of one's consciousness. And this because survival is no longer a problem. Boredom and tedium haunt middle-class existence because only those freed from the necessity of survival can be bored with life. Samuel Beckett's two sad tramps sitting forever under a drooping tree waiting for their lives to begin have no problems to solve but no mystery or spirit to arouse them either.

An ultimate decision each individual can make (if his freedom is broad enough) is that "life is, or is not, worth it," i.e., that the struggle to survive, the struggle to face problems, is balanced in some way by the mystery of life's intrinsic worth. To judge negatively is to choose suicide. Suicide is a spiritual option, a deep one at the level of mystery, for it is a positive NO to the mystery of life. As such it arouses more respect than does a nonoption, a nonchoice, a simple passing out of life "with a whimper" while still within the possibility of life; that is, an option for tedium, for boredom, for lifelessness. Suicide contradicts itself insofar as it affirms one's power to act to end life; tedium on the other hand is an affirmation of nothing, not even the power to end one's life. It is a nonaction, allowing one's world to dictate one's problems; it is far more insidious a disavowal of the mysterious than is physical suicide. It is spiritual suicide accomplished by doing nothing, asking nothing, thinking nothing. Only a creature capable of mystery (one does not see bored dogs or cats) could opt for such a lifelessness.

2. Death, life's inevitable mystery. Death is a mystery of life. Without life we do not stand in awe at death. We do not even consider it (who weeps over the not yet born, or cries for them, or gets nervous for their safety and preservation from death?). For the middle class, death is reduced to a problem (some are led to confusion by modern myth-making about freezing bodies, etc., another example of the rationalization of death; even were such a process manageable, death would retain its mystery, for death is mysterious not because it is unavoidable but because it is bigger than we are). Once reduced to a problem state, death can easily be disposed of and swept away out of sight along with other problems (e.g., mental retardation, poverty). Thus psychiatrist Rollo May can say that for modern, middle-class man, death is pornography; it is the unmentionable. Why is that? Because it is simply a bad problem, a bad trip; it can be "solved" with a little more make-up and softer music and more satin lining in a coffin and more efficient refrigeration. Death must never be discussed, considered, or meditated upon as a mystery in itself.

But a conglomerate conspiracy not to talk about death may well prove far more pernicious than any Victorian or Puritan plot never to talk about sex. For when one shortchanges death, one shortchanges life. They run on one tether. Is it just coincidence that a culture bored with life is also bored with death? Is it mere coincidence that the age of the ennui with life was ushered in by mass slaughters of individuals—children, women, and men—in the World Wars of this century; that is, by the loss of wonder and concern for life? What would be the consequences for a society or for an individual if the decision is fallen into that neither life nor death has a value in itself? When death becomes as boring as life, all mystery will have ceased. Lifelessness will rule supreme, but with a supreme boredom.

There are experts in our midst on the mystery of death. They are people not put off by death as a problem but to whom death remains a mystery constantly accompanying them. Among them is a family who have experienced the death of a child, of one of them, of a living person grasping for life, awakening to its mystery, reaching for its touch and its pleasure and its pain. Do not tell such a family, when their child is suddenly removed from their life, that death is a problem. Do not interrupt the mother as she weeps for the child at night with news that cadavers can be frozen; do not tell his four-year-old sister who looks in vain for her brother to play with that when she reaches the age of reason and is educated she will understand death and learn to resolve the mystery of her absent brother.

When we cannot respond directly to death; when we take it for granted or ignore it by silence or by talking around it (and reducing it to a problem to be solved); when the published lists of traffic fatalities, of war dead, of assassinated heroes, of earthquake victims do not arouse respect for the mystery of death and its constant presence within and without us; when we can no longer face our own death as a distinct moment in our life wherein we stand in the mystery of our life as past and finished; when we can no longer be aroused to working to prevent death, to putting it off, to fighting for life; and when those who fight to survive no longer inspire us—then we are already overcome with the spirit of lifelessness. We are bored and boring.

3. Nature and rebirth as recurring mysteries. Nature itself, the repeated cycles of growth and death and rebirth as manifest in animate nature—trees, wildlife, flowers; the symbols of passionate life we find in the sea and in waterfalls and in rivers; the immensity of mountains—all these are for us also an experience of mystery. They cut so deeply into the unguarded world of our subconscious that they lodge there for centuries as meaningful symbols. How else do we explain the healing experience typified by the sea, the rebirth images of water, the warm, peaceful caresses conjured up by our memories of sunshine? Rousseau speaks for the nature-lover in his *Confessions:*

I arose every morning before the sun and passed through a neighboring orchard into a pleasant path which led by the vineyard and along the hills. . . . While walking I prayed . . . with a sincere lifting up of my heart to the Creator of this beautiful Nature whose charms lay spread out before my eyes. . . . I like to contemplate him in his works.

And Goethe speaks to the pastoral soul: "Do you not see God? By every quiet spring, under every blossoming tree he meets me in the warmth of his love."

It is not enough to say that because so much of our current existence is urban we have given up on the mystery of nature. Quite the contrary; urban man is haunted by a nostalgia for that forgotten mystery which, precisely because nature evokes a mystery, cannot be gotten rid of in his consciousness and subconsciousness. How else shall we interpret urban man's attempts to "return to nature" by way of camping and vacations; by way of parks in his cities; by way of zoos; by way of floral shops and plants in the home (with the paradigm of an urban home being one with a garden on a penthouse roof); with fountains in his city squares; and by the vicarious means of movies and museums and the study of the biological sciences.

Then, too, the urban dweller experiences nature in that most recently exploited of all nature's mysteries, sexual activity. Is it mere coincidence that the sexual liberation on which our society prides itself has paralleled man's movement to the cities and away from nature's everyday presence? Is the human body not the one guarantee a city-dweller possesses (especially if he is poor and cannot escape to the country on weekends) that the mystery of nature's rhythms and tones and swellings and risings and rebirths is still within his grasp? Is it not, then, a pernicious and deadening act to moralize heavily about sexual activity before sexuality is grasped as an occasion for the appreciation of the mystery of nature for the urban dweller? Does one who claims to be interested in the spiritual dare to judge as unspiritual those who seek the mystery of life in human communication expressed in sex? Sex is thus not the mere problem to which state so many would reduce it. It is a mystery as nature is a mystery. It finds a degree of totality and ultimate experience insofar as it is related to an authentic union with another: a common experience to give and to share love. "For many persons it is only, or chiefly, in sexual love that one encounters the category of an end in itself, the category of the sacred. It is from this experience, for many, that religious language becomes meaningful again," observes Michael Novak.[2]

The fact that scientists have begun to "penetrate the secrets of the universe" to a significant degree since Galileo first trained his telescope on the sun in no way of itself reduces nature to a problem. If some scientists sell their soul to consider atomic fission only from the point of view of the problem of war tactics and possibilities, this does not belittle the value of all natural research. Nor does exploration of the planets, even though the billions it costs may be replacing more fundamental human needs of survival back on the home planet. Nor does exploration into the functioning of sexuality such as Masters and Johnson have provided. These researches are antimysterious only to a people who see life and nature as problems and not

2. "The Beauty of Earth," *Religion and Life* (Summer 1968), p. 239.

mysteries. A problem need not be opposed to mystery. On the contrary, scientific discovery very often increases our awareness of mystery by uncovering new depths to our world. Far from spelling an end to an age of mystery, scientific research opens our eyes to the constant and almost overpowering presence of the bigger-than-we-are in our universe. These explorations are neither problem nor mystery, but a *possible* bridge between both realities—if we want them to be. Who could deny that the look on our planet from the moon increased, rather than diminished, our wonder at the uniqueness of our tenuous planetary existence?

4. *Another person as a mystery of life.* Another person is a mystery, a calling of me outside of myself. He or she is a mystery not only because he or she bears within him the mystery of life and the mystery of death and the mystery of nature that he has made over (or that, better, has made him over) within his conscious and unconscious personality, but because to be a person (from the Greek word for mask) is to be a mystery properly speaking. This is why when we meet a person for the first time we do not ask straight off and directly: "Show me your mystery" (which we take to mean himself or herself); we work up to the mysteries in this person's life and the mystery of this person by circumlocutionary probings. Questions of place ("Where are you from?" "Where do you live?"), time (Is this person of my age and generation, or from what world does he come?), work ("What do you do?"), and interest ("Are you a sports fan?") gradually soften up the process of meeting another. But the authentic meeting takes place in insight: perhaps a look into the eyes may be enough for the *revelation* of the person. We say revelation, for this is the way one approaches a mystery: mystery is not arrived at (though it may be prepared for) by our pressured activity. It is revealed, unveiled, opened up for us as a rose in its time and under the proper atmospheric conditions becomes open for the beholder to see. A human person is such

a mystery capable of revelation of self when the time and the company are correct. This revelation is enough to stop one short, to change one who beholds the other.

It goes without saying that those who see others as problems, as body counts, as rungs on one's own private ladder to the heights, or as votes for one's "policies" (always carefully manipulated to kowtow to rather than to attract), or as consumers to be counted and seduced—in short, as usable and useful in themselves—shut out mystery from their lives. In making problems of human mysteries these people run the ultimate risk of reducing their own existence (no less than that of those they manipulate) to a problematic one, a useful one. Once again the consequence of such an option would be lifelessness or tedium with a nonmysterious existence. It is to close oneself forever to the possibility—however distant it may sometimes appear to be from our touch—of intimacy, the sharing of the mysteries of life.

5. *Love as a mystery of life.* Another is a mystery; but the experience that one (who is also a mystery) enjoys with another is an additional mystery. Every person—man, woman, or child —is a beauty waiting to be discovered, uncovered, revealed so that we might respond with our own mystery.

At times we are granted something like a mystic vision. . . . We have found the soul in its seclusion and simplicity—so we think. . . . The vision in fact begins to work upon us; we cannot forget it: we no longer attend to it with voluntary effort, but it forms a part of our consciousness and begins to make us over after its own pattern, as if it were active and we were plastic before it.[3]

A love experience is a mystery unfathomable to exclusively problem-oriented persons. It demands a Yes or a No and will not be denied a response. By it universes are opened up to us

3. William Hocking, *The Meaning of God in Human Experience* (New Haven: Yale University Press, 1912), p. 432.

as we learn anew the excitement of discovery, not only of the mystery which is another and the mystery which is love, but the mystery which is self, the another-for-another. Schelling's man who is *animal amans* (the loving animal) reveals himself and accepts revelation in the experience of love.

The constant presence of the beloved, even though space may separate a couple by thousands of miles, or time by eternity itself after death, is not readily diminished. The beloved's presence is too strongly felt; it is too much a part of one; it is too deep in the air we breathe and the mind we reflect with to be forgotten. We remember mysteries. They are too much a part of us to be forgotten. In this sense Marcel is accurate when he declares that a beloved bestows immortality on another by his love: To say "I love you" is to say "You shall never die." Love is mystery opening up to mystery. No wonder its token is most regularly the granting and encouraging of freedom unto another: the freedom to be his or her own mystery and to live this mystery, loving it.

6. Evil as a constant mysterious presence. Any particular evil is a problem, and man's hopes run eternal that he may conquer this disease by research and save this patient by expert surgery plus luck, or remedy this unjust school situation by law. One dedicates himself to combating this and that particular evil insofar as his expertise and his moment in history present these particular evils to him. But he does not delude himself that he has come to save the world from evil, to rid it of evil. For this sort of thinking would reduce all evil to problem, which would run the risk of reading the history of man's fateful civilizations very superficially, with an optimist's naïveté. It is from this shallow approach to evil that genuine cynicism, that is, literally barking like a dog, settles into a culture or a person so that nothing at all is done about the evil problems that beset any particular moment in history. This approach to evil makes of those who set out to conquer it messiahs themselves; no wonder the plunge from their lofty ideals to their cynicism is so long and so hard. They have expected too much of themselves and too little of the enemy.

Evil, so far as it is mystery, refuses to be manipulated or dealt with by pressure. No law will eradicate racism (though laws are needed to prevent its spread and punish the overt violators); no war will end all wars (and no stockpiling for future untold wars will prevent them); no single commitment to justice will slay the forces of injustice, the powers and principalities that continually—like Minerva's twelve heads—assert and reassert their heads. This sense of evil as mystery is the meaning of Jesus' remark that "the poor you will always have with you." His declaration is not against a socialist welfare system set up as a problem-solver for the poor. It is an observation on the mystery of evil of which poverty is one glaring example: that evil of some sort will continue to haunt mankind.

To say evil is a mystery is *not* to opt for a mystification of evil (as so much Latin spirituality has done). The mystifiers of evil are recognizable by their particular cult. They are ever busy creating evil that they may suffer through either in their own imaginations or—what is worse (but, alas, more common)—in the lives of others whom they love to rule over with spiritual power. This disguised masochism suppressed into a spiritual-ized sadism fools no one and reveals its own contradictions when persons dedicated to ridding the earth of evil problems confront it. This approach to evil has only cozy words to offer the suffering, coming from those who have never suffered authentically; pious platitudes delivered from one-dimensional souls who have a habit of running from evil problems while calling their running a spiritual journey. One cannot resist emphatically enough all efforts by this spirituality to mystify evil, making what are solvable problems (provided one works hard, educates himself to them, and spends himself) the immutable will of God, and reducing the bed for mystery to the scope of their tiny imaginations. This thinking reduces to a state more puny than that of the problem-solvers the mystery of evil that is not contained within any single imagination.

The concept of suffering as a privation of the good and as a matter to be mystified and then contemplated is from an age when hopelessness was the daily fare vis-à-vis most diseases and natural catastrophes. The historical setting for this treatment of evil was the fourth century, which reflected a growing pessimism in the shadow of the declining Roman Empire. The Manichean sect of that period attempted to play down the overpowering experience of evil and despair of the time by deprecating all of life. As a result, other centuries were left with a shallow and ego-centered spirituality, for Christian apologists attacked Manicheism by insisting, as Basil did (A.D. 330–79), that "evil comes from us—man" and the acquisition of virtue can combat evil. "Evil is not a living and animated entity, but a condition of the soul opposed to virtue, proceeding from lightminded persons on account of their falling away from good. . . . Each one of us should acknowledge that he is the first author of the wickedness in him."[4] The father of most western spirituality, Denis the Areopagite, borrowed his understanding of evil from the Manichean period and its sources. Augustine and later Thomas Aquinas would, like their Greek counterpart Basil, emphasize the acquisition of virtue in their moral theology and thereby define evil as an individual's own weakness.

To Jacob wrestling with the angel; to Jesus wrestling with the devil; to Paul wrestling with hostilities, dangers from pagans, friends, false brethren, Jews, Romans, labors, imprisonments, flagellations, shipwrecks, fatigues, sleepless nights, hunger, thirst, cold, nudity; to Helen Keller wrestling with blindness and deafness; to those who have met the mystery of evil in its overwhelming mysteriousness; to those who endured the concentration camps of this century, evil is a positive force in itself—how is evil merely a privation of the good? In what sense was

4. *De spiritu sancto*, PG 29, 27.

the nailing of Jesus to the cross a mere *privatio boni*, privation of the good?

One must ask if this attitude toward evil as an egocentric problem does not betray an optimism and preoccupation of a noble class (both Augustine and Basil were from noble society) who wrote so much of Christian metaphysics (Aquinas, too, was from a noble family). To learn of evil one should put the question to experts on evil: ask a poor black from a small southern town, or a father whose son has just starved to death, if evil exists and is more than just trying a little harder. The idea of evil as a problem (and it always remains in the realm of idea, for such thinking betrays a lack of experience of evil; otherwise it becomes a mystery) was reinforced in a certain flight for the good into Neoplatonic fancy. A search for the positive in life outside of life itself reveals, in spite of itself, the very basic pessimism that initiated the theory in the first place. Luther brought Christianity back to the understanding of evil as a mystery when he insisted salvation is not wrought merely by added good works. Still, his treatment of evil failed to overcome the individual's concern with evil in himself; the mystery of evil grasped in its historic and social dimension broke loose with the French Revolution and the consequent reflections on it, particularly those of Marx.

Today's marvelous improvements in the art of medicine, in the sciences of biological and biochemical research, in surgery, in hospital equipment argue that the first response to suffering is not to tolerate it; today's response to sickness is to put an end to it, not to mystify it or to mystify resignation. Still evil haunts the picture. First of all, because the current cultural situation is still beset with ponderous evils such as the unavailability of hospital equipment and opportunity to the poor and the subsequent anguish many suffer who could never afford hospitals should they take ill; or the chasm that separates the salaries of doctors from the rest of society (not excluding their patients), and the obduration of certain medical unions to healing these injustices. Then there is the fact that many diseases are still far from curable; many persons still suffer needlessly, and in some cases with no medical hope whatsoever. One might make a case that these examples are all of evil as a problem; but the mystery of evil is not in assigning any particular instance of human misery to an incurable land of eternal forms, only in realizing that wherever man walks the earth or other planets his fate is as subject to chance and to randomness and to error and to victimization as is any other existing creature.

I recall meeting a senior in college who told me he was becoming a doctor to work in free clinics in ghetto areas. "It is either that or commit suicide," he said matter-of-factly. He was a person who faced life's mysteries, in particular that which is most conspicious to Americans these days, that of evil. He had no illusions about solving evil as a problem, but he intended to deal with that part of it which is problematical and let the mystery of the remaining evil change him.

Those who can respond to mystery as an evil (who can "see" it, since no logical argument can "prove" its existence) can also respond to life and love as mystery, for evil derives its horror and its tragedy—its power to take us out of ourselves—from our power to love. Evil's source as a mystery is in our capacity for love. If the murder of Martin Luther King, Jr., was an unspeakable horror to so many, was it not because they could love the work and the purpose of the life of this man? The dreams expressed by the wish of "if Malcolm X had lived . . ." or "if John Kennedy had not gone to Dallas . . ." are our way of reliving the mystery of evil and trying to remake it. The power of injustice is great only in relation to the power of justice, as the power of hate is powerful only in relation to what love might do. Our times, which seem so often rife with evil at every turn of a television knob and every glance at a newspaper, must then also be times when the possibilities for the powers of love and of service and of facing life as a mystery have never been paralleled.

7. Vocation as a mystery. Speaking of evil leads naturally into this last of the mysteries of life we will consider. It is the mystery that one experiences when he says, "I feel I want to be a lawyer and work in legal aid," or "I have to write," or "I feel called to minister the Gospel," or "I used to play around all the time until I began my own family and I love them so much I want to do everything possible for them," or "I must make music." All of these instances are what we might call "vocations"; that is, a "being called" to one's work or one's contribution to life. That these callings are mysteries is evident from the very wording in which they are couched. They are convictions, imperatives, that invite one to respond positively. They bring about change in a person's life or attitude toward life. They motivate and dispose him to dedicate himself. They are inescapable. They imply in every case some passivity on the part of the individual; that is, a claim that something happened to him (whether by words or events is incidental) that was bigger than he and drew him out of his tiny world into a bigger one.

Thus the person responding to vocation (and of course one may have several in a lifetime, especially given today's longer and more diverse life spans and opportunities) is also responding to a mystery. In so doing, he is placing himself at the disposal of other mysteries of life, for the zone of influence of a vocation (and one can have a vocation to any role, including totally unknown roles as yet; we must decry that cultural use of the word "vocation" for those entering official religious roles) has no intrinsic limits. No one can limit the positive influence of a good father, a good wife, an able and honest mechanic, a dedicated doctor, a sincere hippie, or a prophetic minister. For what one does as an occupation and where one chooses to live are often far more than problems in our lives. They are the stuff of which mysteries are made, the place and the space in which mysteries that enter our lives will find their home. They are that sacred frontier where we shall be changed. Where we shall live. And where we will pass on life to others.

These mysteries of everyone's life do not exhaust the possibilities of mystery, for as man by his scientific and aesthetic investigations, as well as by his increased technology (so long as the latter subjects itself to mystery or preserving life's intrinsic value), probes deeper into himself and further into his universe, more, rather than fewer, areas of mystery will lay themselves open to man's wonder and amazement. The advancement of mass communications worldwide has brought more and more people of divergent classes and cultures and interests in communication with one another through experiencing of the same mysteries (farmers plowing fields in Africa listened to astronaut landings on the moon at the same time that crowded Parisian television shops showed the pictures and that Americans in their homes viewed them). The spiritual meaning of the communications revolution is unmistakable and still untapped; it must not be allowed to wilt on the vine of technology by prophets of pessimism who want only to retreat into a contemplation of things past. Man does not need religion or cathedrals rising from his fields to remind him of mystery any longer; he is steeped in it from the moment he turns on his television set and witnesses evil at work around the globe to the day he sits in a laboratory and uncovers nature's hidden powers in subatomic particles. We have in this secular Pentecost a potential for a sharing of life's mysteries, as they are happening, on a worldwide scale and for the poor no less than for the rich. This is no insignificant historical turning point, for the poor (including the middle class) to be opened up fuller and fuller to mystery is for them to take hold of their history and to risk everything in committing themselves to a newly won era of justice among men.

The mysteries of life are by no means restricted to an esoteric sect, whether that caste define itself by wealth, power, or religious affiliation. They are the lone bases for union among all men and women of diverse ideologies, for they alone draw people out of their self-constructed universes to a wider horizon of hope and expansiveness where all shall stand freely before the gift and the mystery which is life. Not by competing with others; not by stockpiling things; but by responding to the invitation to experience the mysteries of life does a person become an adult and thereby enter the human race.

CHAPTER 3

Prayer: A Radical Response To Life

Prayer in its primal and fundamental sense, I propose, means *a radical response to life*. I suggest that this description of the prayer-event will bear the burden of the best in former "definitions" and accounts of prayer at the same time that it carries the reality of prayer into the new spiritual age that is yawning before the awakening consciousness of mankind.

PRAYER AS RESPONSE

The English word "respond" derives from the old French verb, *respondre* (to answer), and the Latin verb *respondere* (to promise, to pledge, "to engage oneself"). A response is an answer with a promise to it: not the answer to the question "Will you go to the store for me?" but the answer to "Will you marry me?" The former calls for a reply; the latter for a response. The promise inherent in a response is a pledge of oneself, implying a certain degree of self-revelation based on shared trust and respect. I recall once asking another, "When are you happiest?" The first reply was: "That is a very personal question," but after a long pause for conjuring up response, the individual made the requisite act of trust and was ready to respond. The response marked a new stage, a deeper one of intimacy in our relationship, since clearly the response was both answer and promise.

"Respond" is not a limiting verb: it takes one beyond the ordinary connotations of the word "talk" (thus those who settle for prayer as "talking with God") and beyond the more general word "communicate" (which, like "talk," suffers from an extreme anthropomorphism). Yet we all respond daily to the events and the mysteries that move us. For one responds when one is moved, in some sense implying that passive triggering which is of the heart of the experience of mystery. One does not reply or talk or communicate when he hears for the first time of the death of a loved one: he responds, that is, even if nothing is heard verbally, an acknowledgement of the event is called forth from the depths of his insides. Perhaps the language used is tears. Perhaps, for another sort of appeal, laughter. Or silence. Or a touch.

A response is spontaneous (from the Latin *sponte*, of one's own will): it is free, it is mine. We respond *because we feel like it*, such as a youth does on diving into the sea fully clothed or a child does on spotting candy or bright lights: it is a simple utterance of one's deep feelings. The lack of guile and the lack of planning in such responses characterize those not engaged in schemes to perpetuate one's own existence. Calculation and self-perpetuation are not a part of response; self-expression is. In this sense to be childlike is to be responsive: open and free to express one's own self at the invitation of an event or a person.

A response is simple and directed to the simple; expressing oneself spontaneously is also expressing oneself simply. To be simple is to be oneself uncluttered with ifs and buts, maybes and howevers, calculating all the angles of one's decisions. To respond is to see something with conviction (which is very different from waiting to see it with certitude, such as Descartes and others since him have determined truth must be). Our response to mystery in particular tends to be a response with conviction. A human Yes or No is the most simple and the most convincing response we can make during our lifetime. The simplicity implied in saying Yes or No in response is simple for its depth, for it comes from a place of honesty where one's very being and self-mystery senses its worth is at stake. It is the Yes and No that Luther uttered when he claimed: "Here I stand. I can do no other"; or that Christ spoke when interrogated about his kingship. It is not the consequences that dictate the response (as they so often do the reply) but the inner honesty. It is the No of Bonhoeffer to the Third Reich, the Yes of Mozart to his musical vocation, the Yes of Jesus to his messiahship. Mystery responds to mystery and the simple to the simple.

Response is responsible. There is implied in an adult's answer and promise a capacity to see that promise through. This capacity, not to be confused with duty (which depends on external motivation and sanctions), is motivated from within, where one's certainty lies, and we call it responsibility: the capacity to live up to one's response, to follow through on it. To respond is to ask no compromises and seek no bargains but to accept the consequences of our trust and our promise. It thus throws us into the future, a dark and unknown future, one that we believe can be somehow met and responded to by the depth of our original insight that called for our primary response. Ask the young couple saying Yes to one another in marriage responses, and interview the couple who have lived fifty years together to learn the risk and the consequences of responsible response.

ISRAELITE PRAYER AS RESPONSE TO LIFE

If prayer is, at its primary level, a response to life, it should be borne out in the prayer of great pray-ers of history. Does such a description of prayer do justice to the prayer of the Jews and of Jesus and, if so, in what sense might their grasp of prayer alter or deepen the understanding of prayer we have arrived at as a response to life?

The culture into which Jesus was born, whose language he spoke, and to which he was assimilated was a prayerful culture;

that is, the Jewish people emphasized prayer in their recorded histories in the Old Testament. Not only the Psalms, which are for the most part poetic prayers, but the books of the prophets, the historical books, and, indeed, almost every book that makes up this history of the Jewish people reports praying by these same people. The keystone to Israelite prayer is life. The prayer for life dominates all other prayer.

"For the Hebrew mind, to live meant to have health and joy, strength and success, in short, to be happy."[1] Life is not a concept for the Jews, it is an experience. In fact, the Jews had no word for the abstract concept "life"; their nearest equivalent was *hayyim*, which means the period of life or lifetime. Significantly, this word is in fact adjectival and not a noun. Life for the primitive people of Palestine was first of all survival. The life appealed for in Jewish prayer is not an esoteric mystical experience of a world beyond but an appeal for the daily fare of living and surviving ranging from fulfillment of needs of personal feelings to good harvests to forgiveness and repentance. No dualism of body and soul needs is implied in Israelite prayer, but "what the Israelite asks of Yahweh, over and over again in countless forms and ways is 'life' in the full sense" (Bushinski). A full life, a rich life, a long life are the heart of Israelite prayer.

The experience of the Jews in the Old Testament books is not a vague or idyllic account of life in a sacral or cloistered world. Jewish history is an existential accounting of the experiences of defeat and despair, treachery and deception, politics and love-making, hope and pride that furnish the meaning and the memories of anyone's life. The Old Testament is at heart the story of the *life of a people* and contains within it many stories of peoples' lives. The poignancy of this history and its constant presence in the consciousness of the Israelites, thanks to their oral tradition and the Scriptures, accounts for the fact that prayer and life are not divorced in Israel. "Worship and life

1. Leonard A. Bushinski, "Life," *EDB*, p. 1338.

must belong together, the one as leading to the other and the other as expressing the one."[2] No dichotomy existed for the Jews between the individual's prayer and the nation's relationship to Yahweh. Life was not projected into another world or into another era (though the sign of the messianic times was to be an abundance of life), and any concept of resurrection into another life was vague to an extreme. No, life was what was experienced on earth.

The emphasis on life as a history actually experienced by one's ancestors was a fundamental reason why the Jews prayed with a confidence to their God that was not paralleled in Mesopotamian and Egyptian prayer of the same period. For the Jews based their prayer on the works of deliverance they had experienced in Egypt, in the desert, in Abraham's call from his ancient land: in historical events, in actual life situations of deliverance.

The Jews conceived of their God as one who lives, in contrast to their neighbors' gods and idols who do not live. It is Yahweh who gives life and spirit: "You give breath, fresh life begins, You keep renewing the world" (Ps. 104-30). "The Spirit of God hath made me, and the breath of the Almighty hath given me life". (Job 33:4). Yahweh is the one "in whose hand is the soul of every living thing, and the breath of all mankind" (Job 12:10). "When he withdraws his hand things perish" (Ps. 104:29). "The Spirit of God is the Spirit of creation" (Gen. 1:2). In Ezekiel we read: "See now: all life belongs to me; the father's life and the son's life, both alike belong to me" (18:4). The psalmist sings of the fountain of life: "They feast on the bounty of your house, You give them drink from your river of pleasure; Yes, with you is the fountain of life" (Ps. 36:8–9). This parallel of water and life is what one might expect among a desert people, and it is a rich theme recurring throughout the Old Testament and into the New where, significantly, water—i.e., life—evokes Spirit.

2. H.R. Rowley, *The Faith of Israel* (London: 1961), p. 147.

Furthermore, life came to be identified with the Law for the Jew of the Old Testament. The entire object of the Law is the preservation of life: "You shall keep my statutes and my ordinances, which if a man do he shall live by them" (Lev. 18:4).[3] The just man who observes the Law will be rewarded with life: "I have set before you life and death, blessing and cursing; therefore, choose life" (Deut 30:19). "And now, Israel, take notice of the laws and customs that I teach you today, and observe them, that you may have life and may enter and take possession of the land that Yahweh the God of your fathers has given you" (Deut. 4:1). The sanction for sin is death: "The man who has sinned, he is the one who shall die . . . repent and live!" (Ezek. 14:4–6). "Be good to your servant and I shall live" (Ps. 119:17).

JESUS' PRAYER AS RESPONSE TO LIFE

Jesus was a Jew, and in all the respects concerning the Jewish preoccupation with life in prayer, Jesus was a faithful Jew. This fact carries us beyond the question of his reciting formulas of Jewish prayer and practicing rituals of Jewish worship to his very understanding of the prayerful life. Indeed, in good Jewish fashion, he seems preoccupied with the question of life. He brings "rivers of living water" (John 7:38) and claims that "I have come that you may have life and have it more abundantly" (John 10:10), and that "God is God, not of the dead, but of the living" (Matt 22:32).

Life for Jesus. Just as the ancestors of Jesus were promised life as the fulfillment of the Law, so Jesus (himself called the Law) promises life for those who believe in his word. Life is what Jesus bestows on those who receive him, for he bears the light of life. "He who eats my flesh and drinks my blood lives in me and I live in him. As I, who am sent by the living Father, myself

3. Kaufmann Kohler, "Life," *Jewish Encyclopedia*, 8 (1907):82.

draw life from the Father, so whoever eats me will draw life from me" (John 6:54–57). He gives his flesh "for life of the world" (John 6:51).

Jesus uses the analogy of life constantly in speaking of the Kingdom of God that he announces in his parables. He compares the Kingdom of God to throwing seed on the land; to a mustard seed that grows into a large tree; to a vine bearing branches. The life of which Jesus speaks is not a life unavailable to the poor or the simple. It is bound up in the everyday activities of all men who share the earth: "I do not pray that you take them out of the world" (John 17:15). His parabolic examples of heaven, of sowing, of nature's rhythms, of men at sea, of housewives looking for lost coins, of employer and employee, of family relationships—all point to the stuff of which Jesus considered the Good News made. And that stuff is real life really lived. He spoke in the economic (agricultural and fishing), the climatic, the social, and in the familial idiom of his time and of his companions. This, plus his fierce reluctance to exit from life, demonstrated in his Gethsemane struggle, was his ultimate tribute to the primacy of life. "Jesus without saying so, by his very way of presenting man, shows that for him man's destiny is at stake in his ordinary creaturely existence, domestic, economic and social."[4]

Not only is life the content of his parables, but the very manner of using parables is telling of Jesus' concern with daily life, as Funk has shown in great detail. "It is this element of ultimate seriousness that is implicit in the patent everydayness of the parable. The field which the parable thus conjures up is not merely this or that isolated piece of earthiness, but the very tissue of reality, the nexus of realations, which constitutes the arena of human existence where life is won or lost" (Funk, 155f.). Christ's use of parables, unlike those in the Gospel of Thomas, for example, which point to an ethereal, heavenly

4. Robert W. Funk, *Language, Hermeneutic and the Word of God* (New York: Harper & Row, 1966), pp. 155f.

realm, do "not direct attention by its earthy imagery *away from* mundane existence, but *toward* it."

"Eternal Life." The term "eternal life" has been so frequently and is still so recklessly abused, especially by pulpit preachers, that we should pause to examine its meaning more fully. The synoptic Gospels and the early Paul used the term to signify what they presumed to be an immanent parousia, or second coming of Christ. Experience, however, not only tried the patience of early Christians bent on a dramatic and triumphal salvation, but it deepened their awareness of the person and the message of Christ so that in the later Paul and in John "eternal life" does not signify what is to come but what in fact has already begun. Resurrection is decidedly not about death but about baptism, for it begins at baptism. "When we were baptized we went into the tomb with him and joined him in death, so that as Christ was raised from the dead by the Father's glory, we too might live a new life" (Rom. 6:4).

In John 17 we have an amazing instance of a Gospel writer assigning exegesis of the term "eternal life" to none other than Jesus himself. Eternal life, says Jesus, is knowledge when knowledge signifies belief plus love. The very word employed here in John for knowledge is that used in Genesis to signify sexual union of man and wife. Thus the sense of "eternal life" is intimate converse with the Father, a relationship already begun. "Eternal life" is what all have now (John 17:2).

Not only do the late Paul and John insist on the newness of "eternal life," they even call Jesus "eternal life": "The Life Eternal which was with the Father, and has appeared to us" (1 John 1:2); "You have been brought back to true life with Christ . . . but when Christ is revealed—and he is your life—you too will be revealed in all your glory with him" (Col. 3:1–4). The eschaton (meaning the future victory) has already begun with our lives. (This is further developed in John's and Paul's "glory" theology.) Jesus is reported to say in John: "You study the Scriptures believing that in them you have eternal life; now these same Scriptures testify to me, and yet you refuse to come to me for life!" (5:39). And again, "I am the life" (John 14:6). "Life" becomes a person in John, appearing in the masculine not the neuter gender.

The Father. The one prayer that Jesus teaches his friends begins "Our Father." While the Fatherhood of God is a theme known to the Jews before Christ, the Israelites never addressed God in a prayer as "Father." So much emphasis is put on the Fatherhood of God in the New Testament that Joachim Jeremias calls this "the central message" of the New Testament.[5] The theme recurs continuously: "Everyone who believes that Jesus is the Christ is a child of God" (1 John 5:1); "Think of the love that the Father has lavished on us, by letting us be called God's children; and that is what we are" (1 John 3:1); "For in Christ Jesus you are all sons of God through faith" (Gal. 3:26); "I will welcome you and be your Father, and you shall be my sons and daughters, says the Almighty Lord" (2 Cor. 6:18). The synoptics relegated man's sonship to the last days, but John and Paul characteristicially treat sonship as a gift already conferred (realized eschatology). For Paul the Father has chosen us in love, predestined us to be his sons, and lavished us with his grace so that we may know his will. John emphasizes the Father as a life-giver: "For the Father who is the source of life, had made the Son the source of life" (John 5:26). "But to all who did accept him he gave power to become children of God" (John 1:12). These children alone "know God as Father" (1 John 2:13). What is a father except the one who passes on life? The central message of the New Testament that does in fact "sum up the Christian Faith" is about life, the life-giver, and life-receivers.

But a further dimension, one of "astonishing"[6] intimacy, is

5. *The Central Message of the New Testament* (New York: Charles Scribner's Sons, 1965), p. 30.

6. Stanislaus Lyonnet, *Initiation à la doctrine spirituelle de Saint Paul* (Toulouse, 1963), p. 18.

revealed in the New Testament concerning man's filial relationship to the Father. For Jesus addresses the Father as "papa"
("Abba"), a spontaneity and intimacy toward God that is "something new and unheard of which breaks through the limits of
Judaism." The intimate confidence with which Jesus prayed
"Abba, Father," is passed on to his followers as well. Mankind
inherits Jesus' relation to his Father whether as adopted sons
(Paul) or as sharers in the Father's life (John). So intimate is this
relationship of prayer to the Father that the Spirit itself groans
the intimate word "Abba" (Gal. 4:6; Rom. 8:15) on behalf of
each of us when we pray. Such intimacy in the filial relationship
of man and God is born witness to in the spiritual tradition built
around the theological concept of the indwelling of the Holy
Spirit after the "be in" (einaien) and "abide" (menein) theology
of John. The God to whom Israel now prays in confidence is so
near that he has set up his dwelling within as well as among his
people.

Jesus actually prays in response to life's mysteries. Those moments that are recorded of Jesus in prayer are invariably provoked by real-life situations, by the very mysteries of life we
have discussed. Jesus prayed, was driven to prayer, at critical
life moments so that, in fact, these mysteries alone provoke him
to prayer in the New Testament.[7]

The mystery of his vocation opened him up to prayer at the
descent of the Holy Spirit at his baptism and when he spent
"forty nights and days" in the wilderness. This passage makes
Jesus a new Moses, whose messianic career was just inaugurated
in his baptism, for Moses, too, passed forty days before Yahweh
in fasting and prayer and is the great pray-er of Israel. Jesus

7. Students wanting to investigate Jesus' prayer might begin by asking the
life-situation inherent in the actual prayers of Jesus in the New Testament (Luke
10:17–22 23:43, 23:44–46; Matt. 26:36–44; Mark 15:34; John 11:41–43, 12:23,
27–30, 17:1–26) and in the allusions to his praying (Luke 3:21 f., 5:15 f., 6:12–16,
9:18–21, 9:28 f.; Mark 1:12, 35–39, 6:45–48, 6:41 f.).

frequently felt the need to renew his messianic vocation by withdrawing into the solitude of nature. In the critical task of choosing his twelve apostles, he first spent the night in prayer (Luke 6:12–16). His confession as Messiah at Caesarea Philippi was preceded by his prayer. The Transfiguration scene, recalling his baptismal occasion and the words of Isaiah regarding the annointed messiah of Yahweh is bathed in prayer.

In addition to praying over his messiahship, the mystery of life that we have called the mystery of vocation, Jesus was moved to pray by the omnipresent mystery of evil: "Simon, Simon! Satan, you must know, has got his wish to sift you all like wheat; but I have prayed for you, Simon, that your faith may not fail, and once you have recovered, you in your turn must strengthen your brothers" (Luke 22:31–32). Evil expressed itself in human affliction and sickness (Mark 7:33 ff.) and in face of death—his own—when he fell on his knees, praying and sweating blood in Gethsemane before his "hour" which coincides with the moment of the mystery of his death. And his soul is "sad unto death." Despair at death's power is uttered through Psalm 22:1 on the cross. Death also provokes Jesus' prayer in the case of his friend Lazarus, where Jesus wept before he prayed.

Jesus is moved to prayer at the mystery of others, as when he is thrilled in joy and thanksgiving at the reception of the Good News by the poor and the simple (Matt 11:25–30). And when his apostles succeeded in announcing his messianic vocation (Luke 10:17). People who are causing him pain move him to pray for their forgiveness as he is nailed to his cross of death and agony.

Love is a part not only of Jesus' prayer at Lazarus' tomb, where he prays aloud "for the sake of all these who stand round me," but in particular at the Prayer for Unity of John's Gospel (17:1–26): "I have loved them as much as you loved me."

We conclude that the notion of prayer as response to life is not out of harmony with the teaching and practice of Jesus or of the Jewish tradition but is in fact very much in accord with that tradition's deepest tenets: that the mysteries of life are the warp and woof of authentic prayer. Life is respected as a mystery that carries us beyond the particular moment or particular culture to a God who simply is and in whose intimate presence one dares to stand with confidence. Indeed, with the Jews and then with Jesus, a far-reaching dimension of intimacy is added to the concept of presence to the mysteries of life. It is almost as if to pray is, after Jewish and Jesus' teaching, to stand daily before mystery and before the Giver of Life even in one's most insignificant actions.

Do we conclude from this application of our understanding of prayer to Jesus' prayer that his prayer adds another mystery to those we experience in life? This would be far too simplistic a treatment of prayer, reducing Jesus' contribution almost to the status of a problem. For a better way of putting the question is (as any question about life and its mysteries): What world are we living in? If that world includes a respect for the Jewish tradition or an acceptance of Jesus as the Jewish messiah, then the prayer of Jesus is less an additional mystery than it is one that permeates the other mysteries, offering to life a deeper probing of its mysteries.

PRAYER AS RESPONSE TO LIFE, NOT GOD

It may dismay some that our generic understanding of prayer does not contain an explicit reference to God. The difficulty in talking of God today is that the name, paraded for centuries as the Father of western culture, has lost its meaning within that falling culture. Believers who claim an ancestry to the Israelites might do well to imitate their modesty in the face of Yahweh, whose name the Jews refused to employ more than once a year and whom they refused to address directly. For the Jew, one's name is a sacred trust. To know one's name is to have power over that one. Rightfully, then, they were cautious in pronouncing God's sacred name, for no one holds power over God. Contrast this respect for a name to the use of "God" in American culture, where self-annointed president and pundit alike invoke and preach him. We should not forget that we are a people who have altered the name of God by putting him on our coinage with all the ambiguity that "In God We Trust" implies.

If prayer is a response to life, however, what about God? Consider the story of the prodigal son from the point of view of the father in the story. It is less a story about who the father is than about where and when he is. The final speech of the father in the story, addressed to the prodigal son's "responsible" brother, insists: "My son, *you are with me always and all I have is yours*. But it was only right we should celebrate and rejoice, because your brother here *was dead and has come to life*; he was lost and is found" (Luke 15:31–32, italics added). The answer about "God" in this parable is that he was there all the time. And in a loving, caring way; that is, in sharing all that was his. We have made God over into an image we project of a male deity–whereas our God (to speak analogously) is just as much woman as man.

It has been suggested that in defining prayer as response to life we are eliminating the personal in one's relationship with God. But here we must tread very delicately, much more so than have some recent spiritualities of our near past. This is especially the case for celibates who must constantly resist the temptation to project human personage onto God to substitute for one's voluntary loneliness. God is not a person in our human understanding and need of person. God will not be "used" by our loneliness, though one must add at the same time that God will not "retreat" from our solitude either; he is the one who is "there all the time." He is everywhere all the time. We are invited to seek him and rest with him everywhere, or better, open ourselves up to the fact (the first belief of faith) that he (better, he-she) has sought us everywhere. God can be a personal God without being conceived of primarily as a person.

The so-called "radical" and "death-of-God" theologians (America's spiritual theologians) underline what might other-

wise go unnoticed by religious thinkers to the extent that they
fail to immerse themselves in today's cosmological theories:
namely that Providence is totally Other for man's unconscious
and preconscious today than formerly. In our description of
prayer we are taking the contemporary problem with Providence seriously. We are cautiously refusing to "define" God
or to nominate him explicitly. We are asking those questions
about him in the manner we always get to know a stranger, by
asking first: Where are you from? Where do you live? When can
we meet again? In this modest approach to the God-problem,
the newly defined (and as yet unsettled) concepts of place and
space and time are being studiously respected. We are allowing
for a new understanding of God to emerge. For our new prayer
will yield a new understanding of God, not vice versa. From the
time of Moses to that of Jesus it has been prayerful people,
rooted in the primaries of what prayer is, who have told us of
the hidden and unfathomable God.

Granting an essential modesty regarding one's current talk of
God, and the need to ask Where and When before directly
posing the question Who, does our description of prayer as
response to life offer no guidelines, no hints of the kind of
Providence we shall encounter? We are proposing that the one
to whom we respond ultimately and pledge ourselves in promise is neither a culture nor a nationality nor a race. He-she is
bigger than life with its mysteries and its problems. A mystery
of mysteries, he is everywhere life-giver. God is the lover of life
above all else: its preserver; its promiser; its enticer; its sharer.
"To know God and to live are the same thing. God is life"
(Tolstoy). He is everywhere of it, in it, with it; that is, his presence is everywhere and always present. Providence is a life-
breathing presence and the process of prayer is the process of
coming to realize this. His presence is an immanence (intimacy)
and a transcendence (that which calls us outside of ourselves,
such as love of neighbor and struggle for justice).

But God is useless. Such a Providence performs no routine

machinations on the universe, provides little solace to lonely souls, displays itself on no banners for national crusades. The question for the modern pray-er becomes: Can one believe in uselessness? Can we believe in worth for its own sake? Can we, in Eliot's words, "be still"? The experience of grace, the experience of Providence in our lives, is not an experience of usefulness. It is not a resolution to a problem. Whether the graced moment, the "moment of ephiphany" (Joyce), occurs in sitting by a sunset in an open sea or in seeing our newborn baby for the first time, in our first and surest love experience, we learn that the function of grace is not to do, but first to behold. To uncover. To let be. And, in letting be, we learn that grace is everywhere. Thus resides Providence also, for grace is the breath of Providence.

If Providence is understandable today as everywhere lifegiver, then to respond to life *is* to respond to Providence. For life is our total experience of creation (that which is), and to respond to creation is to respond to the Creator. (We do not take Creator-creation here in a philosophical sense, such as Vatican I took Romans 1:18–25, thus yielding to the ever-present temptation to imperialism based on identifying "creature" and "existence" so that a nonbeliever does not exist. It is for this reason that we prefer the word "life," which does not yet bear the passive and pejorative connotations that "creation" does.) If God is less a problem today, more veiled and more mystery, if God is less useful, then his withdrawnness leaves us an avenue through his creation—which is, indeed, a route our culture is especially equipped to pursue. To respond to life is to respond to the Creator of life. To confront life then *is* to confront Providence. Dietrich Bonhoeffer, from his cell of witness shortly before his execution, remarked that the God of the mystic is the only God contemporary man can grasp. The mystical contribution to God-talk is precisely in considering Providence as Presence, as the following writings reveal:

This incessant prayer now consists in an everlasting inclination of the heart to God, which inclination flows from Love. . . . It is the same as with a person living in the air and drawing it in with his breath without thinking that by it he lives and breathes, because he does not reflect upon it (Johannes Kelpius).

"He Who Is" dwells everywhere. It is only a matter of learning to look into the profound sphere of things, *of everything*. The secret of the world lies wherever we can discern the transparency of the universe. We could say in fact that the great mystery of Christianity lies not in the appearance of God in the universe but in his transparence in it (Teilhard de Chardin).

The spirit world is in fact revealed to us; it is always open. Could we suddenly become as sensitive as is necessary, we should perceive ourselves to be in its midst (Novalis).

The true heaven is everywhere, even in that very place where thou standest and goest; and so when the spirit presses through the astral and the fleshy, and apprehends the innermost moving of God, then it is clearly in heaven (Jakob Boehme).

Religion cannot be defined as an "exclusive relationship with God." It must rather be defined as a specific way of approaching the *totality* (sic) of reality and of realizing this in God's active, absolutely close (and therefore never available) presence (Schillebeeckx).

Whether you eat or drink, or whatever you do, do all to the glory of God. Worship him, I beg you, in a way that is worthy of thinking beings, by offering your living bodies [living bodies means *lives*][8] as a holy sacrifice, truly pleasing to God (Paul).

The contribution of the mystic's God, then, lies precisely in this: that for the mystic, God is ever-present and as an end in himself is always elusive, always nonbeing, never manipulative, always wrapped in mystery where "in me" and "before me" lose their

8. John A.T. Robinson, *The Body* (London: SCM Press, 1961), p. 79.

meaning, a mystery that one can explore and touch but not fathom. The projection of God into the past, so familiar an exercise for the previous culture's God-talk, is not necessary when the gift of the present and the gift of the not-yet are responded to wholly.

PRAYER AS RESPONSE TO LIFE, NOT CULTURE

The question of culture is the question of the world one lives in. A child's world is for him the whole world and how often adults, too, are tempted to childish regression when they want to label their culture, the world they live in, as life itself. As if one's country or one's village were the paradigm of all the possibilities of mystery. We are tempted to render to our culture all the response that we can offer, or, when we become disillusioned with this, to give up altogether, barking like a dog (the sense of being cynical) in rendering a total response to life at all. This is especially the case in a period of cultural upheaval when we want to cling to what we have known and label this clutching at the familiar our response to life. The proliferation of reactionary spiritual movements at times of cultural crises like our own underlines this habitual historic response. But the question persists: Is my world the only culture I can live in? Is life to be synonymous with culture?

Culture is what we and our ancestors have made of life, but that by no means grants it the status of life. Culture is not itself mystery, even though it is the place where we experience mystery and where mystery is evoked all about us. But mystery carries us beyond any particular culture. (Is it for this reason that T. S. Eliot has declared that the only educated person is one who has mastered a second language; i.e., who has surrendered his own pet culture with its symbols and been exposed thoroughly, from the language up, to another?) A culture is relative, for it is a means for mediating life, and there are always others.

The consequence of substituting a response to one's culture for a response to life is borne out in the following epitaph given by a man who proved his point. "What is life? Life is the Nation. The individual must die anyway. Beyond the life of the individual is the Nation" (Adolf Hitler).

Culture alone does not satisfy as an adequate setting for prayer because it is too lacking in mystery in itself and only exists to serve and to support and transmit life, but not to touch it in its mysteriousness. Furthermore, if responded to totally, it will ingest one whole, instead of unveiling more mystery. "This is the nature of *culture*—it is a mine, a deep pool, a complicated and rich universe out of which each person takes what he needs, as *he becomes the culture*."[9] The authentic heroes of our culture are precisely those men and women who, by myth or by fact or by a marriage of both, we come to believe entertained insight which extended beyond our immediate culture to touch universal appeals of mankind and life-lovers everywhere.

At one level we come to realize and acknowledge that the world we live in, our culture, is inadequate to express all life promises. The very search for deeper values for a culture leads us outside of it and leads us to judge an absence and lack of life in our own culture. In all these senses, we can say with Jules Henry that although culture is "for man, it also against him." Which is no different from the counsel of Jesus to his friends (substituting the word "culture" for *Kenosis*) when he declared that they be "in the culture but not of it."

A consequence of recognizing the rivalry between culture and life, each of which makes claims on a person's response, is that a new understanding of transcendence is born. The new transcendence, every bit as mysterious as the former, is that of *substituting human life for human cultures*. How much nearer this comes to a biblical understanding of Providence than that

9. Jules Henry, *Culture Against Man* (New York: Vintage Books, 1963), p. 238.

picture by which man substitutes God up there for life here below, described early in this chapter. The technology man "enjoys" today, especially its power to break down barriers of space and time (the jet plane and television), has also broken into and broken up former cultures. Cultures are a shambles the world over, whether one is living in the Pays Basque (having stood firm for at least seven centuries, it is now succumbing to tourists and television), India, African tribal groups, European countries. Anthropologists scurry to faraway islands to interview natives before their cultures surrender to the invading onslaught of technological man. Besides technology, causal factors in the breakdown of cultures include the availability of education to greater varieties of classes and castes (gradually eroding aristocratic cultures); encroaching ideas, however creeping in the pace they are actually carried out, of democracy (leveling in a political way the "wise man" guardians of a particular culture); ideals of socialism, however jerky be their initial beginnings (leveling in an economic way the billionaire and millionaire moneycrats of capitalism), and, perhaps most vividly conspicuous today, the worldwide diffusion of records and recorders and with them that new language (does not a new culture always begin with a new language?) that appeals directly to the mystery in man, music. One listens and responds to the Beatles whether he be in a Calcutta market, a Senegal village, a Parisian Au Printemps, a New York bistro, or a Moscow subway station.

What we are saying is that the contemporary situation of man and his technocratic culture has qualitatively altered his relationship between problem and mystery, between culture and life. His culture is becoming more and more distinct from his life; more and more relative in his own eyes. The stage of realizing that cultures and not culture (my own world) are authentic mediators of life is the stage of passing from a people devoted to problem to a people capable of meditation (meditation is the experience of seeing singular problems in light of a goal, thus seeing them as capable of being pieces together). The next stage, already launched in certain consciousnesses in this country, is the stage called contemplation: where life becomes synthetic, bathing all of life's particular moments and problems with itself.

Today what we are learning of the world is, finally, The World —not our projection of it, our flight from it, or our exploitation of it. For the television can relate matters more honestly (and therefore more mystery-ridden) than any philosopher of old. The world in its entirety is opening up before our gaze and our hands for the first time in human (and therefore in prayer's) history. This qualitatively new situation will not only make havoc of former contemplative exercises (e.g., that of "being alone before the alone" of the Greeks), but will hold out a promise of new life, that is of a new spirit, to those who reach and search for it and wait upon it. The basic change in modern man is that he is less afraid of life than face to face with it. In the past (even in the days of our grandparents) life was where one lived and where one spoke his or her language. Today life is neither cultures nor institutions but man stretching to the heavens and participating in that effort by live television. It is man in contact with his fellow man the world over by way of common visual sight, music, problems, and mysteries. We are as a race passing from responding to a culture to responding to life itself, where life's mysteries, in particular that of the Other face to face with evil, take precedence over all national and ideological barriers. Thanks to television, says Margaret Mead, youth insists that "morality is going to have to deal with the real thing."[10] So shall spirituality.

But there is a frightening and awesome possibility in this more naked mystery of life and in the reduced importance of culture that man faces today. It is the dark side to the same

10. "A Conversation with Margaret Mead on the Anthropological Age," *Psychology Today* (July 1970), pp. 58ff.

reality. Whereas in ages past we could seek refuge in our culture when our dreams or hopes or works went awry (one could say that, for example, many millions were *not* killed in this century's wars), today there is no refuge from life. There is no culture sturdy enough to stand as a shelter. So there is a negative as well as a positive motivation for the pursuit of life itself in common on this planet: that life is all that binds us together, life with its problems and with its mysteries. The same technological forces that have opened up life to us by destroying cultures have unleashed a powerhouse for the greatest possible evil ever imagined by man: the eradication of life.

This negative imperative, which is as much a part of our future as the positive attraction of the mystery of life (it is in fact the mystery of evil and of death that hovers within and above us), suggests a new kind of mortification for which mankind is desperate. This mortification presents itself as a willing and voluntary laying to rest of our cultures and many of their presumed values. Mankind is desperate and cannot long remain suspended between a culture-oriented and life-oriented spirituality. Margaret Mead has indicated how all experience with analogous cultural upheavals indicates that a people survive only when whole patterns of their culture change at one time. Cultural change is not accomplished piece by piece successfully (note the efforts in Catholic culture to do this and their dismal failure since Vatican II). While many subcultures find themselves in a period of self-criticism and experimentation (e.g., Black Power in the United States) those people who are not first a culture but a people (i.e., a church) must leave what is cultural in their heritage. Now is the time for the Christian Gospel to step beyond its various cultures and cultural periods to support and to work for universal brotherhood. The universal call to assert life as the primary priority *is* the new transcendence.

PRAYER AS A RADICAL RESPONSE

There are numerous sorts of responses we entertain toward
life, but for a response to be prayer it must be a radical one. "It
is a narrow gate and a hard road that leads to life and only a few
find it," warns Jesus. The word "radical" receives rather bad
press these days, but whatever be its emotional connotations, it
is perfectly apt for our purposes. In fact, it is as innocuous as
"radishes" (which derives from the same word) or "roots" (coming from the Latin word *radix* meaning root). If the reader feels
more at ease with root response than radical response he may
make the substitution as we go along.

The characteristics of radical. A radish or root holds its principle
of growth deep within itself; it grows from within, its life is
intrinsic. What is intrinsic implies what is intimate, what one
holds and cherishes as close to oneself. The more intrinsic a
conviction or an answer the more closely it is us. What is radical,
then, is what I cherish as my own.

The radical not only comes from within but it is also directed
(though not exclusively) to within. It is self-critical. It is in-depth
self-criticism and enjoyment before it missionizes to others.
Man's capacity to reflect on himself has classically been invoked
as evidence of his spiritual nature. I suggest that man's capacity
to criticize himself is evidence of the deep roots he is heir to.
William Sloane Coffin defines the radical in contrast to the liberal: "A liberal is a person who thinks other people need help,
and a radical is one who knows we're *all* in trouble."[11] Radical
implies a commitment to oneself being changed at a deep, root
level where intimacy resides.

What is radical threatens those persons (and that piece of the
person of each of us) who cling to a quantitative response to life:
whether by seeking to stockpile millions of dollars or stocks; by

11. "Playboy Interview," *Playboy* (August 1968), p. 135.

measuring security by the number of missiles his country amasses or the amount of overkill his country can unleash on the enemy; by calling economic success an increased gross national product instead of a lessening gap between haves and have-nots. But numerical games are not pleasure-inducing because they are not radical enough. They fail to touch the mysteries of our lives, which are not grasped in numbers. The difference, for example, between having a job and working out one's vocation is that the former is "just a job" while the latter is a mystery to which a person feels himself called "from the depths," in a qualitative and root way. Radical in our use of the term means qualitative. A computer, for all its help in the processing of the quantitative, has little direct rapport with the radical: the roots of our lives where mystery resides. The mystery in us lies deeper than the rational and logical in us. That which takes us deeper than the rational is leading us deeper than the problematic of life into the depths where mystery is at home. A radical response is a response of mystery to mystery. Far from being melancholic and glib-faced when face to face with the paradoxes of life, what is radical in us laughs and weeps, dances and thunders—but does not itself become a problem in its encounter with mystery. It becomes more fully mystery itself. To be radical is to be mystery-rooted, planted as a radish or other root plant is planted, in the soil of the very mysteries of life. Perhaps this is one reason (and not only Marx's reason that they are oppressed) that the poor are often more prayerful than the wealthy: because their lives are less occupied with problems (since the quantity and abundance that procreates problems is less available to them) and have more time for mystery.

A response to life is radical when it is life's response (that is the Spirit's *through* us: it is not simply our response. "The Spirit too comes to help us in our weakness. For when we cannot choose words in order to pray properly, the Spirit himself expresses our pleas in a way that could never be put into words, and God who knows everything in our hearts knows perfectly well what he means, and that the pleas of the saints expressed by the Spirit are according to the mind of God" (Rom. 8:26–27). A response is radical, then, which is outside, because deeper than, the daily experiences and judgments of men. It is, in a word, bigger than we are.

What is bigger than we are challenges us to be bigger than we have been. The radical response becomes a courageous and magnanimous sort of response to life such as one finds in the lives of Jesus, Francis of Assisi, Martin Luther, Teresa of Avila, Malcolm X, and Cesar Chavez, to mention a few. "The best fruits of religious experience are the best things that history has to show. They have always been esteemed so; here if anywhere is a genuinely strenuous life" (James, 204). Thus to respond radically is to respond with a bigness of heart and a courage to the qualitative in life. "The great thing which the higher excitabilities give is *courage*; and the addition or subtraction of a certain amount of this quality makes a different man, a different life" (James). The radical response is not a mushy wish; it is a certain desire, a conviction that will effect change or be defeated in the process. It is a willingness to accept defeat, to make a mistake, to lose oneself (and even life itself)—but to do this for a great cause and with a full effort, rather than to let things be and wither in the process. It is a plentiful response to life, one uttered out of one's abundance, not out of one's smallness and scarce feeling for life and its mysteries.

The radical, because it is big-hearted and deeply rooted and deeply felt, requires a certain amount of folly in the everyday judgment of what is and is not foolish. "I am a fool for the Lord," exclaims Paul, and the logical and rational, the expected and the expectable, that which machines and men who are programmed like machines predict, would find no category for the person who responds to life in this way. But the child within the adult, the nonrational and the foolish *are* a part of life even if clowns are less apparent with the advent of technopolis.

The directions of radical. Happily, our English language has superb expressions for the discernable directions of "radical." The first direction is that of "becoming rooted in;" for "transcendental" need not only mean what is above (up), but also what sinks so deep that it more profoundly upholds the daily: and what is vertical does not mean only what goes into the heavens but also what attaches itself into the earth with strong and energetic roots. We become rooted into the pleasures and enjoyable places and persons and memories of the moments of our lives where we have learned to savor life and its mysteries. The second direction is that of "rooting things up" or "uprooting." This is the war cry of that famous man of prayer of Jewish history, Jeremiah, who felt himself called to "root and to uproot," and is recalled in Jesus' words: "Any plant my heavenly Father has not planted will be pulled up by the roots" (Matt. 15:13).

A tension in our life-response asserts itself in the dispute between our desire to enjoy life and our drive to improve it and to share it; in the warfare between allowing oneself to be changed and aiding the situations of others so that they might be changed; in the strife between receiving, seeing, listening, being, touching, dancing, singing, and expressing love by way of peace; and our giving, doing, acting, fighting, making, arguing, and expressing love through anger. The poles of the dialectic that we call becoming rooted in versus uprooting has classically been called that of mysticism versus prophecy (cf. Heiler). The reason that the process of life-response is a dialectic that remains suspended in tension is that the roots of our uprooting are built right into those of our being rooted in.

The dialectic, or rooting-uprooting, that is the arena for an adult's spiritual life is first experienced in adolescence. The search for self-identity and for the experience of intimacy with others and intimacy with God after the shock of loneliness in leaving childhood and preparing for the hard adult world is the budding of natural (as opposed to tactical) mysticism. The search for identity and intimacy is a search for roots that one can plant. Another stage to the search will be that of setting out, confident of one's roots, to create justice for one's fellow man even by uprooting where necessary. It goes without elaboration that those intent on "instructing" others to prayer do so by encouraging the mystical and prophetic possibilities from adolescence onward. This stage constitutes the only authentic Christian pray-er's adulthood because it is love. Neither stage is ever arrived at fully; the dialectic is constant, as Heiler indicates in analyzing the spiritualities of Luther, Zwingli, Calvin, Fox, Bunyan, Pascal, Kierkegaard (his omission of Francis of Assisi, Dominic, or Ignatius is not intentional): "the devotional life of by far the larger number of religious geniuses represent in varying degrees a mixture of the mystical and prophetic" (227). The fact that a radical response is of its very definition a constant, unresolvable dialectic argues that it alone is capable of responding to the mysteries of life that bathe our conscious and our subconscious much as water flows through the gills of a fish. Only at this root level does prayer become constant, and therefore adult prayer.

The strenuousness of prayerful persons' life-responses indicates that the rooting-uprooting dialectic is decidedly not a compromise (how much radical energy is washed down the drain by mediocre compromises to lukewarm positions that are no more prophetic than saying nothing) between prophecy and mysticism, so that one sort of balances off the other as two cards placed edge to edge. The thrust of the assassination of Jesus is, after all, that they killed him, that his prophecy went too far. ("Imprudent," one could hear official guardians of mediocrity advising.) No, the essence of radicalism, once its dual dialectic is granted and integrated into one's response, is that it strives to go all the way—in both directions. That is to say that one sets himself or herself to fighting for justice 100 percent and for enjoying life 100 percent.

It is not only one's personal odyssey from childhood through adolescence to adulthood that reveals the mystical-prophetic theme of the spiritual; this rhythm is found in a people's social as well as personal history. Some thinkers today (Heidegger, Marcel, Schillebeeckx) contend that technological society following on industrial society produces an "anti-contemplation complex." That may be the immediate result of technology, but spirits in contemporary America indicate that the attempt to eliminate the roots of our lives made by the technological society in fact are compelling more and more reflective persons to assert these roots. From the oppressed rises the spiritual.

Some decry current society as overly active as opposed to contemplative. But the historical change over the past two hundred years has not been so much a flight from contemplation to operation as it has been from prominence given to mysticism (in a time when lack of technology and rigidity of social institutions and limitations to man's thought and capacities encouraged a passive approach to life) to prominence given to prophecy or criticism of life's mediators (in such a division of directions: both Freud and Marx have alerted us to the latter direction, for the essence of prophecy is criticism and it will always be social whether criticism of the hidden consciousness or of the hidden cultural economic forces). In previous ages a vocation to prophecy was a very restricted one; that is, the possibility of radical change in any social institution or the understanding of any was severely limited. What is basically new is that education in science and technology have drastically altered this situation so that today every social institution, every "idealistic" state, has the potential to change. In this sense the key tension is not contemplation versus operation but change actively taken (to uproot) and passively taken (to become rooted in). The categories "active" versus "contemplative" have lost their meaning. As Santayana insists, contemplation does not lie in not acting but in living when one acts. Prophecy and mysticism best describe the spiritual awakening of the present. The spirits of almost demonic excitement and terror, no less than the marvelously life-giving ones unleased in our culture today can only be discerned from the vantage point of mysticism and prophecy, of enjoying life and sharing it.

In previous world-views the radical was kept distant by subject-object dichotomies and by preoccupation with survival problems. But today the mystery and mysteries of life—from unimaginable injustices (we see races led to ovens of extermination; children dying of hunger while the "average" middle-class citizen in some countries is sated with food) to undreamed-of sights (one recalls visions of the earth relayed in living color from the moon)—are naked and open for all to respond to. The democratization of western life, as incomplete as that process is two hundred years after the American and French revolutions, has still accomplished this much: the immediacy of mystery for most persons in western civilization. This situation is opposite to those who would decry our age as spirit-less or without religious vision. Never before has such a percentage of a culture been face to face with mystery, and, therefore, with the spiritual that demands a radical—that is prayerful—response. Never before, then, have the possibilities of an authentic spiritual renewal been so promising and so widespread.

The understanding of prayer as a radical response to life suggests the following lesson. That a new commandment has been given to us: thou shalt love your life with all your strength and energy, growing daily in appreciation of the joys of life; and you shall allow and aid where possible your neighbor to love his and do the same, using common norms of justice to determine life's priorities. Live to make life livable: fighting when necessary, learning by whatever means possible, having a good time when you feel like it, respecting life's mysteries in an active, not a passive manner. In short, love life—and do whatever you want.

CHAPTER 4

Prayer as Radical Psychologically: *Mysticism* (Becoming Rooted)

In understanding prayer fundamentally as a radical response to life, we are maintaining that prayer, from the personal or psychological point of view, is before all else the process of responding to life. It is not any process of living and responding to life but a radical response. In this chapter we pursue the question of what it means to respond to life in a radical way psychologically.

PRAYER, THE PROCESS OF RESPONDING TO LIFE

Prayer is a psychological reality to the extent that it is the process of the individual growing, becoming, and being changed. Prayer is a process because, as we saw in Chapter 1, it is constant; but for us humans, only processes are constant. In this sense prayer is the process of rerooting oneself, or better, ourselves. From a personal point of view the essence of prayer, even of a mystical experience, is the way we are altered to see everything from its life-filled dimension, to feel the mysteries of life as they are present within and around us. The process implies change. "Let your behavior change, modeled by your new mind. This is the only way to discover the will of God and know what is good, what it is that God wants, what is the perfect thing to do" (Rom. 12:2). To say that one's capacity for prayer is one's capacity for being changed deeply is to detect a certain passivity in prayer. Van Buren indicates this when he says that the language of faith implies "that something *has happened* to the believer, rather than that he has done something." Prayer is the process of becoming alive, of rooting ourselves into life.

Where shall we be rooted? We detect four areas of personal or psychological rooting and rerooting: awareness, freedom, appreciation, and attitudinal conversion. None of these root responses excludes the others; none is a safe plateau that, if reached, shelters us from the others. Like the tide, these responses will come and go as different times and seasons of life and of life-happenings awaken us and call them out of us.

1. Awareness. To respond radically to life's mysteries we must be aware of them or know them. Prayer is first of all a growing in awareness of life and its mysteries. It is growing into life, learning to feel and breathe and sense life. Sir William Osler observes that "half of us are blind, few of us feel, and we are all deaf." Awareness is seeing buildings and teapots and not just thinking "shelter" and "drink" but form and shape and beauty and curvature. It is hearing a sparrow sing and identifying one's own voice with another animal's. Awareness is the capacity to be *wholly* where one is and to be alert to the possibilities of enjoyment and wonder, awe and beauty, goodness and peace exactly where one is. Recall that Peter sought to prolong the experience of the Transfiguration by erecting a tent and camping on the spot, as if the place on the mountainside and not the place in his mind and heart was the enduring locale of the Transfiguration event, whereas Jesus advised returning to the city.

Awareness concerns place but also time. Awareness is of the "now." We either sense the suffering in the eyes of a person we shake hands with for the first time or we do not. We either let today's sunset into our bodies and persons today or we do not. The Martha-Mary story, which has received so fanciful an interpretation by spiritual writers for centuries (being called an allegory of the contemplative in opposition to the active life), is in fact a story about enjoying the now. Mary has developed her capacities of enjoying the now, and in this sense has "chosen the better part," because the everyday problems of keeping house are readily put aside when the opportunity for enjoying a mystery (in this case the presence of a friend, Jesus) presents itself. Mary is open to the now; Martha is too busy. We cannot postpone awareness to a more convenient time or for a mood when we feel we are ready for it any more than we can postpone mystery to tomorrow. To be aware in a prayerful way is to be sensitive to the pathos of the present. An aware person grows in realizing that every day bears its mystery: every person one meets, every event in the news, every feeling felt deeply by oneself. We open and grow in readiness to respond to that mystery and thus to becoming aware. An aware person is eager to behold life now "with as much poignancy as possible."[1]

To be aware of the now is not to live exclusively in the present, oblivious of the past. It is to bring the past and the future to bear forceably on the present. A return to the past as well as a vision into the future is concerned with the roots, not the topsoil, of our memories and our hopes. A radical awareness neither despoils the past nor escapes from the future for one's roots are invariably grounded in those times. It is conscious that the only way to root or simplify the present is to refresh and inform it by recovering the simple from other times.

The keystone to growing awareness is growing in honesty. The dishonest person who has cut himself off from some reality already and goes about trying to cover up mystery in himself or smother it (jealousy) in others is losing his capacity for aware-

1. Berne, *Games People Play* (New York: Grove Press, 1964), p. 180.

ness. He who is honest is aware because he is constantly on the
lookout, like a sentinel in a watch tower, for possibilities of
growth and of falling deeper in love with life. But to be looking
is also to admit that one needs to grow, that one is lacking in
some way or other. The difference between the prayer of the
Pharisee ("I thank you God that I am not like this man") and
that of the publican ("Lord, have mercy on me a sinner") was
the difference between one who was convinced he needed no
alteration of a root kind and he who was open to being changed.
We have an instance of honest awareness in the case of a contemporary pray-er of great depth, Malcolm X. In his autobiography he recalls,

The hardest test I ever faced in my life was praying. . . . bending my
knees to pray—that *act*—well, that took me a week. . . . I had to force
myself to bend my knees. And waves of shame and embarrassment
would force me back up. . . . For evil to bend its knees, admitting its
guilt, to implore the forgiveness of God, is the hardest thing in the
world.[2]

The core of dishonesty is to resolve not to learn from others; not
to ask questions of a fundamental kind regarding oneself and
one's ideologies, not to want to change. Whereas the teaching
of Jesus, present not only in the parable of the publican and
pharisee but also in the startling demands he made of his followers—"Leave your father and your mother" (recall that his was
a preindustrial society and therefore a culture where all tradition and mores came from one's family and elders)—is to surrender one's inheritance. And he not only taught this, he lived
it.

Some theories of prayer have gone to dangerous extremes in
emphasizing honesty as self-criticism. A mystique of humility
defined as self-abnegation characterizes the following reflection
from Claude Bernier, a seventeenth-century French Catholic

2. *Autobiography of Malcolm X* (New York: Grove Press, 1966), pp. 263f.

spiritual writer: "What is a creature? He is a collection of every corruption, of poverty and of incapacity. What he must be encouraged to do is to humiliate himself, annihilate himself, plunge himself into nothingness and live in a perpetual fear of fragility."[3] This negative sort of spirituality has been a particularly influential one in American Catholic circles of religious where some young women were taught to memorize this kind of spirituality as recently as a few years ago. Yet masochism has no special home in a prayerful person's world, spiritual writers to the contrary notwithstanding. "Insofar as there is such a thing as religious masochism, it is always a perversion" (Marcel, *M of B*, II, 100).

To be humble is to be truthful, especially about oneself. This truthfulness applies just as much to one's talent (recall how Jesus roundly chastises the burial of talents in his parable of the talents) as to one's limitations. Authentic pride is the cornerstone for a spiritual humanism. The more humanistic strain of Christian spirituality (cf. Gregory of Nyssa, Thomas Aquinas, Francis, Dominic, Teilhard de Chardin) takes seriously the Genesis teaching that man is created in the image of God. "We, with our unveiled faces reflecting like mirrors the brightness of the Lord, all grow brighter and brighter as we are turned into the image that we reflect; this is the work of the Lord who is Spirit" (2 Cor. 3:18). Honest pride is authentic humility.

If awareness is openness to the great in life, then among the great mysteries is one's own capacity for contribution to life: its birth and rebirth, wrestling with its enemies, its love of a unique and personal kind. To be honest is to be oneself and to grow in understanding and respecting one's own unique contribution to life. "To be nobody-but-yourself in a world which is doing its best, night and day, to make you everybody else—means to fight the hardest battle which any human being can fight, and never stop fighting" (e. e. cummings). Yet the "mystery of grow-

3. *Ch. ins.* I, 1.1, ch. 2.

ing," the same writer assures us, "happens only and whenever
we are faithful to ourselves."

One who is honest is searching, and in this sense to search is
to pray. It has been said that prayer "is essentially to seek
God,"[4] when "to seek" has the biblical reference *(zeteo)* of the
merchant seeking for fine pearls or the housewife seeking for
the lost coin. It is well to recall that in these parables the search
is less into one's own soul than it is a search outside of oneself
into the real world of seas where pearls reside and kitchen floors
where lost valuables lay hidden. The search is a search for the
valuable: a search for the living. Saint Teresa asks her sisters if
seeking is not the heart of praying: "Strive like strong men until
you die in the attempt, for you are here for nothing else than
to strive." And we can ask whether they who seek are not they
who pray.

If prayer is the process of a man admitting to himself and to
others that he needs changing, then prayer is also the process
by which the Spirit, who is none other than the breather of life,
the greatest mystery, is allowed to enter the world. It is the
opening of the door to the Spirit. For the only possibility of
there entering a new direction and a new insight and a new gift
into human history is through the consciousness (better, subconscious) of man. And that entrance is the entrance of the Spirit,
provided access is laid bare by honesty and a welcome is laid out
by searching for fuller life and greater awareness of life. "Search
and you will find; ask and it will be given to you."

Prayer of honesty, then, is the avenue to a process of becoming aware. To be radical psychologically is to be honest all the
way so that layer upon layer of masking, that is, dishonesties,
must be stripped off, peeled off, ripped off, gently coaxed off. (Is
it not in this sense that the struggle with certain layers of human
experience, for example, masochism, is to be understood in
examining the lives of pray-ers of past epochs? A Heinrich Suso,

4. A. Hamman, *La Prière*, I (Tournai: Desclee, 1957), p. 140.

for example, admits of growing out of a need for flagellations in Christ's name.) So integral is honesty to prayer that one can say that the honest man or woman is already a prayerful person. Jesus surrendered his life not out of blind obedience (when obedience meant, as it has for centuries, obedience to a patron or cultural-hierarchial pattern) but out of an honesty that he expressed as obedience to the Spirit. It is the Truth that makes one free, and Jesus' death was unavoidable to the extent that he refused to waver on his conviction about his vocation. He would not play games with this mystery before Herod and thereby save his skin; he would not dishonestly cover up what to him was a mystery greater than himself. If a one-word description of prayer must be had, "honesty" is far more to the point than "conversation" or "communication," for it implies the process and the mystery clothed in intimacy (to be honest is to be intimate—with self and others) and courage that prayer bespeaks.

2. Freedom and letting go. If becoming aware of the mysteries of life is what frees one, then we are asked to respond radically to this freedom. And this response to freedom we call letting go. One is free to respond to life's mysteries as one feels and cares to. Mystery does not predict or program a response. Freedom and uniqueness are at the very core of the response, for a response is *my* response.

The process of growing in freedom, which is the prayer process, is the process of growing in the freedom to *be* oneself. The Father into whose image we are made, according to Judeo-Christian belief (and after whom we are to be patterned as "perfect" as he, according to Jesus) is He who is. "I am who I am" or "I am who I will be" (Exod. 3:14). He is the monotheistic deity who alone is who he is. We, too, are invited then to be who we are. And this freedom is so radical that it urges us (as it does the Father) to encourage the freedom of others, encouraging them to be themselves, putting on no airs, no cover-up, no dishonesty for us. Does there exist any more authentic test of one's claim to have experienced freedom than one's capacity and willingness to encourage the freedom of others? Is our God not one so eager for our freedom that we may even choose to reject self, others or God? This is how the Spirit—who, as we have seen before, works through man, the only creature open to mystery—breathes freedom, "where the Spirit of the Lord is, there is freedom" (2 Cor. 3:17). The freedom of which we speak implies freedom to make a mistake and even to fail in the eyes and judgments of our culture—as Christ did.

The conviction that freedom is at the very core of the prayerful process is nothing new to Christian thinking as such (though various schools of spirituality have certainly done their utmost to squelch it in recent centuries). Paul calls this the very purpose of our redemption: "Everyone moved by the Spirit is a son of God . . . being freed . . . to enjoy the same freedom and glory as the children of God." (Rom. 8:14, 8:21) We find the same emphasis on freedom in particular among the spirituals of twelfth-century Paris, the spiritual precursors to the great humanist revival of twelfth- and thirteenth-century Europe. Liberty is the very definition of contemplation in that century, and Richard of St. Victor defines contemplation as "the penetrating attitude of a free spirit, suspended with wonder towards the sights of wisdom"; and Ernst Käsemann, in our day, insists that Jesus means freedom because "the freedom of God's children . . . is his revelation, his glory."[5]

Gabriel Marcel, by insisting that prayer is about man's freedom and God's and by rejecting causality as a category for this process, follows in the footsteps of his twelfth-century countrymen. For him God is "Freedom who arouses freedoms in order that Love may be possible". Our moments of wonder at our own freedom are themselves moments in the process of prayer

5. PL 175, 117A, 67D; Käsemann, *Jesus Means Freedom* (Philadelphia: Fortress Press, 1970), p. 41.

no less than our wonder at evil in the world and the scarcity of freedom are also moments of prayer. In prayer we let ourselves go, that is, trust our freedom in the presence of the mysteries of life. Far from providing a security blanket, prayer as the experience of freedom is also the invitation to experience life, to enter into its mysteries with hope and confidence. Freedom is the choice to risk, and prayer, the process that opens up more and more clearly to us our freedom, also confronts us with these risks.

3. *Appreciation and savoring.* A psychological response to life's mysteries is not only one of becoming aware to them and of experiencing one's freedom in their presence (for if mystery does not free us from ourselves and our compulsion to *do* so that we might *be*, what will?). Prayer is also an appreciative response, one of thankfulness and therefore of enjoyment. First we shall inquire how thankfulness is a radical response, and next, how enjoyment is a form of thankfulness.

"Existence is a strange bargain," James Gardner has written, "life owes us little; we owe it everything." And so it is. We are all—the panhandler in the subway, the conductor of an orchestra, the harassed executive, the skeptical student—receivers of life. Even if we choose to exit from life, that is our choice only because we first received life and the very momentousness of that decision to hasten our exit carries with it its power because it is turning our back on a gift; it is saying no to a freely received and freely given occasion to live. To see life as a gift (and therefore to be grateful for it) is to see life as a multisplendored opportunity; to see life as too short to meet all the people, taste all the pleasures, love all the lovable people, witness all the world's cultures, waterfalls, and sunsets: in short, to see life as a gift is to be thank*ful,* full and overflowing from the roots up at the invitation life extends us. But to be so full, to experience such plenitude, is to experience what is actually part of us at a root level. To be thankful is to be radical. For thanks will not be contained. Nor will it measure itself out carefully. It simply gushes over in spontaneous, free, and sometimes foolish response.

From the point of view of those who believe in Jewish and Christian Scriptures, life is indeed a gift. The Christian word for life is "grace," which means thanks in almost any language except English (and if it means thanks it implies gift). To believe is to believe that life is grace-filled: that every creature is a beauty to be uncovered, discovered, waiting breathlessly to turn us on. To accept the first chapters of Genesis—that creation is "good"—is to believe that life is a gift. A gift is freely given and is therefore not to be manipulated, but uncovered and discovered. In human circles this means we are invited to uncover the gifts in one another, the charisms as Paul calls them. To see life as a gift is to see life as nonmanipulative. And it is to see all life's mysteries as themselves holders of greater life possibilities. Thanks is the response one makes to a gift and, if one feels deeply that the gift is of value in itself (i.e., nonmanipulative), then his thanks are deep, he is thank*ful*, and this is itself a radical response to life. It is prayer.

But how does a person say Thank You when he receives a gift? Is it in words such as "thank you"? No adult would say so. When an adult receives a watch from a friend, he demonstrates his appreciation by wearing it. If your aunt gives you her picture you hang it on the wall, at least when she is visiting. The Jews of the Old Testament period were wise in this respect for they had no word for Thanks; only praise to their God sufficed for thanks. But praise is first of all a life fully lived. A receiver of a gift demonstrates his appreciation by using the gift or by enjoying it as the case may be. This is the sense of the parable Jesus taught when he told of the servants with five, two, and one talents. Here we learn that one is knighted a "good and faithful servant" for responding in kind by investing—that is, using—the gift of talents given. He who only hoards the gift (because "I was afraid") is a "wicked and lazy servant." Thus, one best

responds thankfully to life as a gift by living it fully, by enjoying
its multiple possibilities.

But responding to life does not mean one is condemned to
do life (as one speaks of "doing the town"). Life, since it is a
mystery, calls first of all for what we let it do to us. Our response
even of thanks may be a response of freedom to be. Thus we
savor life. We enjoy it. Like an evening at an ocean's sunset, or
a glass of wine, or a quiet conversation with a loved one, or a
meaningful act of love. To do nothing and simply be is itself
radical, especially in a work-oriented culture. To enjoy life is to
say Thank You for it. One does not need explicit words in this
response any more than one needs words in other theories of
prayer where so much stock is often put in silence before God.
Silence before life is often our deepest and most radical response. To receive is to say Thank You, and reception often
requires silence and savoring. One expresses his gratitude by
saying "Yes, I accept your gift and shall enjoy it immensely."

But one does not say Yes only in silent seriousness and alone.
One says Yes to life by living joyfully, spontaneously, freely, and
intimately. This doing we call play. Playing is thanks. In a sense,
because of its spontaneity, it is the most radical form (psychologically) of responding to life, just as laughter is often our sole
outlet for responding to the incongruities of life's paradoxes and
contradictions. Play is a sort of dance of laughter, a laughter
with one's whole self laughing. As such it is a root response to
life's mysteries. To play and laugh is decidedly not to manipulate or use the gift of life, but solely to respond to it. To laugh
together, that is to celebrate, needs no defense as a means of
giving thanks *(eucharistein)* so long as it remains root-oriented
as sometimes happens when families get together to celebrate.
Needless to say dance is a part of such a celebration (cf. David
before the tabernacle). If we call prayer laughter with God it is
not only because we become aware of the good life God would
have us enjoy in laughter, but because in our honest awareness
we have already learned that to know oneself well (as to know

another well) is to smile. The test for love is the capacity for persons to laugh at one another as to love oneself is also to laugh at oneself. To laugh is a radical response to mystery. To laugh together marks a high point in our spiritual lives. God is the Great Laugher who laughs with as well as through us. The "mirth" of God, G. K. Chesterton warned us half a century ago, is too great for (unspiritual) man to long endure.

But we have claimed that there is a fullness in a radical response of thank you, a plentitude and passion in our answer to the gift of gifts, which we call life. And so there is. Why is it that Jesus was such an extremist that he went and got himself killed? He was often an extremist: making friends with prostitutes, eating with the wealthiest and the simplest, raising a fuss in the Temple, pronouncing about himself in the synagogue, taking on the political and religious powers of his culture when he could merely have lived life calmly and pacifically. Jacques Barzun has written that "what is characteristic of life is the thing that antedates and denies convention. . . . This is no doubt why saints and apostles more often consort with thieves and prostitutes than with bankers and aldermen." He goes on to point out that William James and others who have reflected on the matter believe that "the sinner is closer to God than the conventionally good man because life is given us as a passion" (in James, vi). This passionate response to life is a love for life. Hocking observes that "there is a love of life in us which we never let go. But that love of life, if we can discern its true nature, is at bottom a love of God: it is that mystic thread which in the ground of the soul is never broken." Life, says Teilhard, is our very "appetite for being," the "*dynamic* milieu that embraces and super-animates" all forces; note the emphasis on dynamism, a "zest for existence" in Whitehead's phrase.

Where there is passion for life there is risk, the willingness to lose it. "Unless a man first die. . . ." "Life cannot be played without stakes: life is inseparable from some form of risk" (Marcel). To live radically is not only to be honestly aware and to be free and to be thankful and enjoy life; it is to throw oneself into life with a passion, without rational measure or calculated figuring on the outcome. To respond to life radically is to love it passionately—and to assume the burdens and risk that implies.

4. Attitudinal conversion. The fourth "stage" in our psychologically radical response to life which is itself a prayer is the process of being changed that we call conversion or change of heart. This is not being changed as a Democrat is converted to Republicanism or as a Packer fan is converted to being a Bear rooter. Psychologist William Grier writes that "the ultimate power is the freedom to understand and alter one's life."[6] Such a conversion experience, one that is so deeply rooted that it attacks one's own basic attitudes, was an experience for Malcolm X (and from then for the whole Black Power movement in our country) when, in Mecca, he felt a tremendous "impulse to pray" and then began for the first time "to reappraise the 'white man.'" It was with this conversion experience that he determined that the black American must respect all men. To undergo conversion is to see the mysteries of life in a new light, as Malcolm X saw life's enemies, in this case the white American, differently. Because it changes attitudes, conversion is a "high-water mark of one's spiritual capacity," that is, it marks a culmination of the honest awareness, the freedom, the appreciation one entertains toward life. The effect of conversion, observes William James, "is to bring with it a changed attitude towards life, which is fairly constant and permanent although the feelings fluctuate."

The Old Testament prophets spoke out on the need for attitudinal conversion as an integral part of the process of prayer. This inner conversion took precedence over any prescribed prayers.

6. William H. Grier and Price M. Cobbs, *Black Rage* (New York: Basic Books, 1968), p. 60.

> I hate and despise your feasts,
> I take no pleasure in your solemn festivals. . . .
> But let justice flow like water,
> And integrity like an unfailing stream (Amos 5:21–24).

And Jesus cites this same theme: "Go and learn the meaning of the words: 'What I want is mercy, not sacrifice' " (Matt. 9:13). "Oh, you Pharisees! You clean the outside of cup and plate, while inside yourselves you are filled with extortion and wickedness. Fools! Did not he who made the outside make the inside too?" (Luke 11:39–40). The call for "repentance," for "change of heart," for "conversion" *(metanoia)* is the heart of John the Baptist's preaching and later of Jesus' as well. Conversion of one's inner attitudes becomes a test for authentic prayer, not vice versa (John 5:10–15).

But the occasion for conversion is not an exact moment or a precise experience here or there: it is itself a process, as is evident from Paul's having to struggle with his attitudes after his striking moment of conversion marked by his toppling from his horse. Years after his dramatic fall he could recount that "now is the favourable time; this is the day of salvation." This is, that the day of change of heart, of conversion, is *always*. Life is short (2 Cor. 6:2) and the aware and the free and the grateful will respond radically by being ready for deep change in their attitudes now. Note the emphasis in Jesus' parables on being prepared or ready: which, more than a call to the second coming, is a manner of speaking of the attitude of awareness and readiness toward conversion that is a prayerful attitude. Jesus and the Old Testament are in full agreement, then, that religious experience is not of the essence of prayer, but change of heart is. You may have the former without the latter, but that is false prayer. The change of heart is not a once-and-for-all occasion but a process of living out one's life openly, an attitude of being ready to alter one's attitudes.

Jesus responded to his life radically by loving radically. He

was above all a radical lover who loved his own "to the end,"
who freely laid down his life in a manifestation of his love which
was a love "greater than which no man can have." He extended
his love to the poor and to the rich; to his friends and to un-
knowns and foreigners (the Samaritan woman at the well). The
self-offering that his love required in the end was an absolute
giving. "All absolute giving . . . is a self-sacrifice" (C. J. Jung). As
if his life and death would not be enough to convince his followers of the radicalness of human love, Jesus left his teaching as
well. "Love your enemy"—that is the summit of his ethical
teaching. My enemy is he whom I fear most. For Jesus the true
radical in a psychological sense is the lover; he who gets outside
of his former attitudes—especially those of fear—based on inheritance ("He who leaves father and mother . . .") and accepts
his newly grafted attitudes of loving to the end. Reputation does
not seduce the lover, nor do ideologies deceive him. Mystery,
the mystery of the other, is always the first value no matter what
the problems of the moment.

The conversion to becoming a radical lover, continual process
that it is, is buttressed by the other processes of prayer: namely
awareness, which instructs one in how others have become
radical lovers and how therefore it is possible (cf. Malcolm X's
conversion noted above); in *freedom,* which is the only source
from which the fountain of love can spring and continue to
spring through a lifetime; from *appreciation,* which encourages
love because it encourages one in the fact that he is loved: else
why this gift called life? called grace? In appreciation one learns
that he is loved and in *conversion* one takes this image of love
and makes it his own. That is, he accepts it radically. He clings
to it and will not let it go. So confident does he grow in his
awareness and appreciation of love that he realizes that the
reason prayer must be a process and not a momentary word is
that God has only one word to speak and that has been spoken
once and for all. Only the Spirit of Truth, eager to touch the
subconsciousness of all men, can carry on this word. It will only

be by love; and then only if one has let open his attitudes to allow this new breath, this new life, this new Spirit to blow.

Our conversion to love—the radical message of prayer preached by Jesus (and by the Jewish prophets before him)—is a conversion to a new life; not in the sense that we have here another mystery (also called life) to be juggled along with the mystery of life and the mysteries it bears in its train, but new in the sense that we see life (there is only one life) in a new way. It is the same life with the same problems and the same mysteries. But by love, which is prepared for by our change of heart and attitudes and is "poured forth into our hearts," we cannot respond spontaneously and deeply, that is radically, as formerly. Jesus did not suggest a "re-birth" to Nicodemus because he was depressed by the mysteries and the possibilities of the life he met around him; he suggested it because to respond in a radical way (psychologically this means in a loving way) to this life, we have got to see it in its fullness: in its plentiful possibilities for good and for evil, for peace and for war, for justice and for injustice, for love and for hatred, for eternity and for never. The faith of which Jesus spoke is a new, increased awareness to see not new life but life in a new way—in a loving way, with its possibilities for redemption. What distinguishes this life from any other is our capacity to distinguish the Presence of the Author of life, of the Spirit, constantly breathing new life and hopeful mystery.

But Jesus was radical. He did not say that our mind or our reasoning needed rebirth but ourselves. If in our process of growing into life we also grow into this fact, that we are wholly new ourselves, then a message of newness, of spontaneity and bigness, is born with us: the radical becomes incarnate because he "makes all things new" from their depths. "Put off the old man which is corrupt, and, with yourself mentally and spiritually remade, put on the new man, the new life, and the holiness which is not illusion" (Eph. 4:22). New relationships and new shuffling and sifting of life's mysteries will occur because a new life, a radically lived life, is being breathed by a Spirit too big to stop.

Awareness, freedom, appreciation and conversion of one's attitudes fill out the process of prayer from the point of view of a personal, psychological response. Each is radical in its turn and none is a final word spoken definitively in response to life and its mysteries. Instead, the cycle is always and with every stage of one's life reexperienced, though with a new and deeper understanding. "We shall not cease from exploration / And the end of all our exploring / Will be to arrive where we started / And know the place for the first time" (T. S. Eliot).

MYSTICISM, A MATRIX FOR PRAYER

What we have outlined as a radical personal and psychological response to life may conveniently be understood as our definition of authentic (as opposed to tactical) mysticism. The increased interest in mysticism characterizing so much of American culture (especially among youth cults) can be a viable force in the renewal of authentic prayer throughout many cultures and subcultures. Whether one defines mysticism as Dr. Rufus Jones, "immediate awareness of relation with God, or direct and intimate consciousness of the Divine Presence"; or with Thomas Aquinas, "experimental knowledge of God," such as one hears of in the psalmist's words, "taste and see that the Lord is good" ("Through the gift of sanctifying grace", reports Aquinas, "the rational creature may . . . enjoy the divine person himself"), the very ambiguity of the term should not put us off.

I define mysticism in a general way as our capacity for enjoyment. More precisely, as our search for the beautiful (and its search for us). Our growing in authentic mysticism consists of our sinking our roots more and more surely into the beautiful. Any search for beauty in life is in some sense a mystical search. Given the vast subject that mysticism can be, its application here can be restricted to the following propositions:

1. I agree with William James that mysticism is part of certain persons' temperaments and psychological constitutions (he talks of "the mystical faculties" of human nature and how some persons are better equipped than others for mystical experience [297]). Thus there *is no need for a mystique of mysticism;* it will assert itself in proper and healthy (i.e., creative) channels if it is allowed the time and the encouragement to develop. Here I take a strong stand against those schools of "tactics" who intend to "teach" others in mysticism. Mysticism is not a learned reaction; it is a matter of life-response. (Marcel insists that the teaching of prayer is "absurd.")

2. Mysticism itself has to be redeemed. The Christian ideal, as present in the life of Jesus and of Christianity's great models from Paul to Dominic to Francis to Luther to Teresa, is not one of pure mysticism but of channeling and using mysticism for purer ends of prayer and of prophecy. So essential is this to the correct interpretation of prayer in the Old Testament and the Gospels that one can ask: *Can* one be a mystic and a Christian? My reply would be, if prophecy is uppermost, yes; if not, no. In that case mysticism is a flight from the Gospel demands. When mysticism interferes with prophecy, there is something thoroughly un-Christian about the mysticism. Sick mysticism will be identifiable for its flight from history, an opiate substitute for justice just as Feuererbach and Marx claimed it was. The temptation to be swallowed up by one's psychological response to life in mysticism comes to the fore in extremist cults à la Charles Manson no less than in adolescents whose verbal interest in God may substitute for facing ethical demands of adulthood (not only teen-agers are adolescents but enormous numbers of adults, too, including clerics!). A flight from the historical and prophetic, a constant danger for mysticism, is why both Paul Tillich and J. B. Metz feel mysticism offers no ultimate resolution to the spiritual dilemma of contemporary civilization. Mysticism cannot resolve meaninglessness, insists Tillich, because "it plunges directly into the ground of being and mean-

ing, and leaves the concrete, the world of finite values and meaning, behind." And Metz insists that "Salvation, the object of the Christian faith and hope is not private salvation. . . . His (Jesus') cross is not found in the intimacy of the individual personal heart nor in the sanctuary of a purely religious devotion."[7]

3. Still, there lies within the human psyche certain faculties for enjoyment of life and even of the life-giver. This mysticism, if encouraged in its native state (as opposed to being foisted on those not prone to it) and purified in light of prophetic demands; if encouraged by teachers and institutes dedicated to enriching life's mysteries, would contribute generously to a new stage in life-response that is prayer. The way to encourage authentic mysticism is to encourage its sister, prophecy. For the radical lover moves beyond the world of the personal and psychological. The prayer process, which goes on as long as life keeps beckoning and we remain open to become aware, free in our response, grateful and ready for conversion, is a movement toward love, however imperceptibly it may rise from the roots within us, that will set fire to the earth. It alone will root us for that terror of vocations, the winnowing and the sword-reeling that love demands: the call to "prepare the way" for the coming of the Spirit of love by lowering the mountains and raising the valleys—the mountains of ideology and petrified attitudes, the valleys of broken spirits and smothered visions, which perpetuate the reign of injustice on earth. Thus psychological prayer nourishes as much as it feeds on prophetic or social prayer. As the roots are allowed to grow, so goes the uprooting.

7. *Theology of the World* (New York: Herder and Herder, 1969), p. 260.

CHAPTER 5

Prayer as Radical Socially:
Prophecy (Uprooting)

We have maintained that to pray is to take life seriously (not to be confused with taking life lugubriously, as we saw that play and celebration are serious responses to life and its paradoxes). And that the personal process of taking life seriously is the process of becoming radicalized; that is, rooted into life, allowing life itself to reach us as the experience, the ultimate mystery and possibility. In Chapter 4 we suggested that the truest form of expressing gratitude for life is to enjoy it, to savor it. But there is a thorn in our side in our process of life enjoyment that the writer E. B. White captures in this observation: "If the world were merely seductive, that would be easy. If it were merely challenging, that would be no problem, but I arise in the morning torn between a desire to improve (or save) the world and a desire to enjoy (or savor) the world. This makes it hard to plan the day."[1]

THE SOCIALLY RADICAL AS PROPHECY

The call to improve the world we understand as a radical social response to life. We call this type of response *prophecy*.

1. *International Herald Tribune*, 13 July 1968, p. 16.

This term is not an arbitrary one, but boasts authentic origins
in the Old and New Testaments. All of the prophets of the Old
Testament are men of intense prayer, a prayer that brings them
face to face with their perilous vocation, which is one of bearing
witness to the demands of the Law of Yahweh, a Law written
on men's hearts no less than in their oral tradition. The greatest
among the praying prophets of the Old Testament is Jeremiah
—at least we possess more references to his prayer than to other
prophets' prayers. (Probably this is because we have his bio-
graphical narratives in the third person and his autobiographical passages, the "Confessions of Jeremiah.") He faces God in
prayer over his vocation to being a prophet:

> "I have appointed you as prophet to the nations."
> I said, "Ah, Lord Yahweh; look,
> I do not know how to speak: I am a child."
> But Yahweh replied,
> Do not say, "I am a child."

Go now to those to whom I send you and say whatever I
command you. (Jer. 1:5–7) He intercedes for others in his prayer
and prays a full and typical Jewish prayer. He suffers in his
prayer, revealing a tormented soul torn at its roots: "Why is my
suffering continual, my wound incurable, refusing to be
healed?" (15:18). "A curse on the day when I was born, no
blessing on the day my mother bore me!" (20:14; cf. Job's la-
ments).

But Jeremiah's prayer is not restricted to the uttering of his
personal feelings, however deeply felt. His prayer is woven into
his prophetic vocation, his calling "to tear up and to knock
down, to build up and to plant" (Jer. 1:10). The prophet is
primarily one "who is called"; "who proclaims" the word of
Yahweh that He is transcendent but near, special to Israel yet
God over all nations (Amos 1–2); a God of love (Hosea), justice
(Amos), and holiness (Isaiah), who promises a new kingship and
life of peace from a messiah descended from David. The com-

mon notion that a prophet is one who predicts the future is not accurate. The announcement of the messiah was only a small part of the prophet's role, and what is more, an announcement is not a prediction. A prophet does not deal in predictions about the future but in bringing about the future and thereby in announcing the coming of justice by doing justice. If prophets possess foresight it is as a rule because they experience life deeply, becoming in tune with life's roots, and they are more sensitive to the evils and other mysteries of life that all men share. "Foresight is primarily insight" and "predictions, however concrete and true to the historical situations, are primarily a dramatization of spiritual judgments" for prophets of the Old Testament and for Jesus.[2] The prophet's root psychological experiences express themselves in his uprooting vocation. One's social response to life follows (though not necessarily chronologically) from one's psychological response. "The mystic in action is the prophet," declares Hocking (439).

Jesus' life and death are prophetic prayer and his teaching on prayer, as we have seen, is decidedly not Dionysian or Platonic mysticism but prophetic for its insistence on inner moral conversion of a radical kind. His teaching in parable, which as we have seen calls forth a radical psychological response by its parabolic mode as well as by its message, is also prophetic, for it shatters the piety of the culture of which he was a part. "The parable as a paradigm of reality unfolds the logic of the everyday world in such a way that it is: a) brought to the surface [psychologically radical; awareness]; and b) shattered [prophetic]" (Funk, 194). A parable of its very make-up is "an affront to the 'logic' of piety, but good news to the dispossessed because they have no basis for a claim on God. The latter but not the former can accept the 'logic' of grace" (Funk, 197). Thus Jesus announces his message by way of a shock technique, "for with-

2. C.H. Dodd, *The Parable of the Kingdom* (London: Fontana Books, 1961), p. 55.

out parables he did not speak to them," and the purpose of his message was in fact to change people radically into lovers. That Jesus anticipated trials of a social kind for those who preached his word and fashioned their response to life after his own is evidenced by his warnings to his followers (Matt. 10:34). "Do not suppose that I have come to bring peace to the earth: it is not peace I have come to bring, but a sword."

Jesus places himself in the prophetic tradition of "tearing up and knocking down": "For I have come to set a man against his father, a daughter against her mother, a daughter-in-law against her mother-in-law. A man's enemies will be those of his own household." And he warns that his followers will continue the prophetic tradition: "I am sending you prophets and wise men and scribes: some you will slaughter and crucify, some you will scourge in your synagogues and hunt from town to town . . ." (Matt. 23:34). None shall escape the call of the prophet, a social call that will raise the ire of the guardians of society. Prophecy is not done away with in Jesus' time though he has inaugurated the "last days." Rather, the prophetic vocation is everyone's who receives the word of Yahweh. There is an uprooting of religion implied in Jesus' replacement of the Temple (invariably and in all its forms the symbol of religion) by himself, and a recovery of the sense of this prophetic claim among believers aligns them with the early Christians who came to realize that they were the Temple.

Were it not for the history of Christianity (the Crusades, the Inquisition, the constant harassing and persecution of the Jews as scapegoats), the concept that Christian prayer is socially radical (i.e., holds justice and love in highest priority) would require no explanation or defense. But the fact is that prayer has come to mean not a preparation for the prophetic but a replacement or even sublimation of it. In a nonprophetic (and therefore one-sided) response to life the psychological becomes the social, usurping the former's rightful place. Piety and social intransigence go to church regularly hand in hand. In this way, love of neighbor is confused with "being nice" (anger, one's very capacity for moral outrage, is a sin) and questions of justice are conveniently considered outside the realm of one's prayer life. In contrast, we have seen that the only real "answer" to prayer is a changed person on the one hand and a changed people, that is a changed world or culture, on the other.

Prophecy as a prayerful response has played a very small role in the spiritual and theological literature of recent centuries. Bouyer's series on the *History of Christian Spirituality* equates spirituality with mysticism and Congar's *History of Theology* has no references to prophecy at all. Perhaps the reason for this lies in the basic immobility of medieval life (buttressed by a Platonic worship of the immobile); or in too much emphasis on praying to a God of affective love (celibates—who dominate so much of the writings of spirituality—were the only ones to develop a nuptial mysticism as the epitome of prayer experience); or in the preference of more prophetic personalities for spending themselves for others rather than composing tracts on God's intimacies à la the more introspective; or in the past three centuries of Christianity being overly influenced by a Cartesian definition of truth that is neutral and therefore has nothing to do with the prophets' outrage over injustice. As modern, industrial society emerged with its promise of greater freedom to greater numbers, prayer seemed to surrender whatever spirit of prophecy it still possessed and to turn into itself so that mysticism entered the picture as a special science alongside (even separate from!) theology. Since a theology of conceptualization was more and more coming to the fore in this age of rationalism, and since theology divorced itself from other sciences which were in full swing and progress, spirituality ran to a corner and there sucked its thumb in lonely mysticism, at least until Vatican II.

But the relationship of justice and prayer—prophecy and prayer—has not always been so roundly neglected in Christian spirituality:

Then he told them a parable about the need to pray continually and never lose heart. "There was a judge in a certain town," he said "who had neither fear of God nor respect for man. In the same town there was a widow who kept on coming to him and saying; "I want justice from you against my enemy!" For a long time he refused, but at the last he said to himself, "Maybe I have neither fear of God nor respect for man, but since she keeps pestering me I must give this widow her just rights, or she will persist in coming and worry me to death."

And the Lord said, "You notice what the unjust judge has to say? Now will not God see justice done to his chosen who cry to him day and night even when he delays to help them? I promise you, he will see justice done to them, and done speedily. But when the Son of Man comes, will he find any faith on earth?" (Luke 18:1–8).

We are told this parable on justice and injustice is about "the need to pray continually." Might such a spirituality once again set fire to human history by way of inflaming men's and women's consciousnesses?

SOCIAL PRAYER AS A WRESTLING WITH THE ENEMIES OF LIFE

Prayer is not only a response to life of a root kind by way of savoring and enjoying life but also by way of confronting life's enemies. In a real sense the history of prayer is the history of power in a praying community and in the world at large. For prayer is the attitude one takes toward evil powers; it is a battle; it is man's struggle with evil whether one considers the wrestling of Jacob with the angel, the grapple between Jesus and the devil in the desert; Paul resisting arrest; or Malcolm X resisting racism in white and black America. A person by way of prophetic response is not guaranteed a rule that will distinguish what is mystery from what is problem in the area of life's enemies; but by intuition he grasps it, learning respect for what is mystery and engaging in unrestrained battle for what is problem. Prophetic prayer will grasp a person, as we saw Jeremiah was grasped, in the depths where his vocation lies, so that he knows with an assurance that not even he or she can shake that his calling is to fight the battle in this place at this time however veiled the consequences may be.

What then are the enemies of life of which we speak? They are those powers that would reduce life's mysteries to problems in refusing to say "yes" to the mysteries life harbors. Ivan Illich writes: "All authentic movements for change must be concerned with freedom and human liberation. They are an affirmation of life itself against the oppressive forces of exploitation: cultural, ideological, psychological and sexual."[3] Without lingering over details we must further specify these enemies of life. We have already talked of life's quantifiers, who would convince us that life is arithmetical at its roots: we savor it by multiplying our money, our time, our status symbols; bigness is value because it is measurable as bigger than our next competitor. Thus competition is an enemy in American culture from the very time we are introduced to it as children, being taught that our worth as an individual is somehow dependent on our being better than others. Any force that inhibits the freedom of another when that freedom is the actual growth of the individual touching on his psychological roots is an enemy. "It is the freedom to understand and alter one's life, both individually and collectively, which has been denied the black man" (Grier, 60). Thus racism of any kind is such a powerful enemy of life. It not only prevents the free, spontaneous, and deep response of another's life (i.e., prohibits prayer), but it interferes with the same in the life that harbors it.

Another enemy of life is a patriotism gone berserk, a marriage of political convenience that takes precedence necessarily over the importance of persons. Such was the marriage of church and state that took place after the Reformation (witness

3. *The Bread Is Rising,* #4, pp. 9 f.

the "religious" wars that followed). Any commitment to a culture that takes precedence over commitment to life, as, for example, a clericalism that lives in a bygone clerical world (always self-revealing in its language, topics of conversation, humor, basic concerns), is equally an enemy of life—not only in its power to dry up individuals otherwise capable of living life, but for its implicit support (by lack of criticism) of the status quo. Every human being roots himself: the question is what world he roots himself in and whether this world puts human life, individually and communally, as the ultimate priority. As Marx has noted, "to be radical is to grasp something at its roots. But for man the root is man himself."

It is evident that the starving and poor and uncared-for sick are being deprived of life. All forces that prolong this agony are enemies of life. So, too, rapers and polluters of streams and air and fields are destroying the mystery in nature, with its capacity to bring peace and conjure up refreshing symbols of life and rebirth. Those who make death an unmentionable or who exploit it to their financial advantage are equally engaged in making war on life and its mysteries. So, too, those who would exploit another by sexual abuse—whether that came from using another sexually (the *Playboy* philosophy) or from sacralizing sperm (as the ecclesial inheritors of a tradition of fear of the body and mystique of virginity would do). Comfort or security for its own sake (held up as a goal in itself) is a sure-fire enemy to life and its mysteries, for it presupposes that at base life is a problem. A guilt that renders a person or a people helpless to alter themselves or their surroundings is a manifest evil spirit in middle-class America. So is loneliness, which eats at the souls of so many materially confortable persons—young, old, and middle-aged alike. Who can count the ravages that fear has wrought by instilling a paranoia and compulsion for security in a people so that the need felt to construct weapons of destruction in abundance is so much more heeded than the need felt to beautify and make livable one's life and the cities and homes where life is lived out?

These are a few examples of the enemies of life, the spirits of evil, as we experience them in our culture. To let them lie is to encourage them; to refuse to say No to them is to join them in their rejection of life's mysteries, for it is to run from one's own personal mystery which is one's prophetic vocation. This would be the ultimate in prayerlessness—what Fosdick calls "the only unforgivable sin." Everyone called to prayer, to life in the spirit, is called to prophecy, and the projecting of our personal prophetic vocation onto "heroes" is nothing less than a surrender of our spiritual life. A prophet might serve us as a model, but in the spiritual life there are no heroes. Each adult person is alone before his or her unique prophetic possibility and response to life's enemies. Every adult has a prophetic vocation.

JUSTICE, THE PROPHET's GOAL

If the person changed radically in a psychological way is changed into loving radically, what does this mean in the social and historical arena? How is it affected and how does it become effective? Love, whose meaning varies with cultural circumstances, has a history. Does love have a name today?

I suggest that love today means before all else justice. Justice is the direction given to love. For the only way to love God is by loving one's neighbor; but the only way to love one's neighbor (apart from "being in love," which limits one's understanding of neighbor) is by justice. Very simply, he who says he loves his neighbor but ignores justice is a liar. And he who says he loves God, whom he does not see, but hates his brother, whom he does see, is a liar. Here we are at the heart of prayer, the heart of psychological conversion (to being a radical lover) and social response to life. Justice is the zone of all prophecy, the matrix for prayer, for one brings life to the fore by introducing justice.

Justice is the first concern for those who love life, and he who prophesies, that is speaks (i.e., acts) on behalf of the one who is Life, who speaks in the Spirit and the Spirit in him, speaks against injustices, in particular against those enemies that rob others of their first gift: life. Injustice, fortunately, is not an abstract concept, but is highly arithmetic in its initial grasp. A recent study by the Brookings Institute, for example, reveals that in America today the lowest fifth of the population economically scrounge for ·3.2 percent of the national income while the highest fifth get 45.8 percent. The top 1 percent of U.S. families get 6.8 percent of the income, or more than twice as much as the bottom 20 percent. Prophecy becomes only too down to earth when it judges powers and principalities, thereby angering and upsetting the present condition and order of things. Yet Marcel warns that "what we call the normal order is, from a higher point of view, from the standpoint of a soul rooted in ontological mystery, merely the subversion of an order which is its opposite."[4] For the Old Testament prophets Yahweh is the "non-God," the "one whose demands are not essentially in terms of this or that religious practice, but of righteousness and justice between men."[5] A new order is implied in the prophet's message, an untried one, a love of enemy, an embracing of the poor and dispossessed, the *anawim*, which yields a "peace that the world cannot give."

One loves his enemies by way of justice. Justice is a condition in which a person or a people can be aware of, develop, and create their freedom. Thus to preach justice is to face the powers as they are, all those powers that may be massed to rob another of his freedom. It is threatening the status quo with being uprooted. But the key to justice is that it is a balance; it is measurable; it is "a rationalized balance of power against power."[6] This is why prophetic prayer—the announcement of justice when there is none—has to do with the poor and the

4. *Philosophy of Existentialism* (New York: Citadel Press, 1968), p. 42.
5. Herbert McCabe, "Priesthood and Revolution," *Commonweal* (September 1968), p. 622.
6. Rosemary Reuther, *The Radical Kingdom* (New York: Harper & Row, 1970), p. 23.

suffering: because one is poor when he lacks power. The struggle for and on behalf of the poor is the struggle for power. In this sense the struggle of the prayerful person is as much a struggle for power as it is for peace. Indeed, the latter can only exist authentically (due to a reasonable order) on the basis of the success of the former struggle.

This struggle for power and for justice that is the prophetic response to life begins at home. It is by changing one's own being that one makes a contribution to justice in the world as Malcolm X saw so forcefully: "Where the really sincere white people have got to do their 'proving' of themselves is . . . where America's racism really *is*—and that's in their own home communities; America's racism is among their own fellow whites. That's where the sincere whites who really mean to accomplish something have got to work" (495f). This capacity to work with one's self, and to avoid projecting prophecy on those away from one's own, parallels that characteristic of psychological radicalism that we saw begins with self-conversion. Ivan Illich notes, "liberals are always willing to fight other people's battles—to march in Selma, to contribute to SNCC, to move next door to a black man. But they are unwilling to confront themselves, to confront their own unfreedom and the oppressive structures in which they live."

This need to prophesy to one's own is imperative not only because this is characteristic of a root response (to change self, metanoia, and conversion) but also because one cannot in fact alter radically another's life. One does not change other people except by love—and then only each person changes himself. One does not teach another person; one only learns by teaching himself. D. H. Lawrence sent up the cry of prophetic prayer: "God of justice, when wilt thou teach the people to save themselves?" What one can help alter is another's life-situation, another's relation to the powers in a culture. Then the other is free to change himself or not.

The prophetic task is a *critical* work (from *kritein*, to judge):

a work of judgment, of "testing the spirits." Not unlike Socrates the gadfly, one responds radically to life by criticizing the powers that dictate to others what the limits or even the definitions of their lives are. Prophecy is a critique of the institutions of one's time, and as such is a regular part of spiritual revivals, whether one speaks of the twelfth-, sixteenth-, or twentieth-century religious revolutions. Social criticism is left empty-handed if not directed where injustices become incarnated, that is, in the institutions that man might have erected for service but that time has worn into counter–living forces. Prayer then becomes a critique of our ideologies, a reflection and meditation on them, the moments of putting them to a test, putting them into question in the presence of a vision of justice.

The prayerful disposition is the willingness to put all into question. The negative way of prayer need not be restricted to looking on God as an unknown or not yet known: it applies to looking at the whole of our world that way. To remind oneself and others of what they are not yet is to set the stage for radical transformation. This Not Yet is prophecy and prophetic prayer. The critique of prayer may extend even to mystery, for perhaps within a mystery there lies a problem that will only emerge as a problem if mystery is probed. To refuse to probe mystery out of excessive respect is superstition. It can be said then that I am in the world only to the extent that I criticize it. Otherwise, I become *of* the world. For to be uncritical is to be *of* the world. Jesus, among others, has advised that one be "in, not of the world." To say No to the mediators of life at a certain time in history is to say Yes to life. Those engaged in authentic criticism, expecially when that criticism is addressed to themselves and to their own institutions, are engaged in prayer.

The more a person engages in authentic uprooting, the more demands are made on his roots and the more deeply rooted must he become in an ultimate belief that life is a gift. Social uprooting without continual personal rerooting runs a lethal course, for then life and its mysteries (not the least of which is other persons) is in jeopardy of becoming a means. Social fanaticism runs rabid and unchecked when the social substitutes for the psychological. Totalitarian regimes of whatever stripe cannot tolerate pleasure and bear witness to a historical repetition of this sort of fanaticism. Ideology, not life, becomes the ultimate object for man to wonder at and divine, usurping the role of mystery. Life becomes coextensive with one's own outlook on the world and the malaise called messianism fills the psychological void. Thus the need for the kind of root trust and belief that Jesus recommended to the prophets who were to follow him: "Do not be afraid of those who kill the body but cannot kill the soul. . . . Why, every hair on your head has been counted. So there is no need to be afraid" (Matt. 10:28–31).

SIGNS OF THE TRUE PROPHET

It is evident that inherited guidelines cannot suffice for discerning a true prophetic spirit, since a prophet is by definition one without precedent. He or she brings what is new. Not every claim to being "radical" is such: if *radical* is now taken in place of *spiritual* then we must "test the roots (spirits)" still. What are the tests, that is the signs, we can look for in true prophecy?

1. Personal rerooting. One sign we have already indicated is, of course, that a socially radical response to life implies a psychological response as well. For man does not live by anger alone nor for anger alone; nor does he live solely to strive. He who does is rightly called a fanatic, for he misses life—its worth and its joys. Prophecy undergone by a radical lover is a rejection of the extreme that is a fanatic messianism (a messianism Jesus thoroughly rejected). Christian prophecy presupposes love and is subject to it (cf. 1 Cor. 13:8). The roots for the prophet's uprooting lie deep in his psychological response to life, a love of life and an appreciation for it that expresses itself first in enjoying life, next in being deeply converted by it in its favor, and finally in becoming a radical lover.

2. *Reluctance.* Another sign of the prophet in each of us is a certain reluctance, a shyness to accept the burdens of one's prophetic vocation. We find this reluctance in Moses, who sought excuses for not leading his people; in Jeremiah and Isaiah and the other prophets. Is this why Jesus was so frequently driven to anguish in prayer over his messianic vocation? This reluctance stems both from a desire to put savoring life ahead of fighting for it and by a realistic intuition into the price the prophet usually must pay. But the savoring is tasted so deeply that one is "called"; that is, he is urged and compelled to share what he has tasted, to improve the opportunities of others to savor life, and to preserve what is of such immense value within that mystery. He or she accepts the calling reluctantly and with absolute certainty that his preaching is addressed to himself as much as others and must begin at home.

3. *Creativity.* A further sign, one that is intimately related to the previous one, is creativity. The prophet issues new life by his radical response to life: he creates. Creativity is related to reluctance because "creative power is mightier than its possessor." It is an authentic criterion for the prophet's word because "disease has never yet fostered creative work" (C.J. Jung).[6] To be radical in one's social response to life is to be creative. "The worshipper does not merely sustain, but creates" (Hocking, 440). The radical responder to life is driven to creation, to sharing that life of which he has drunk so abundantly.

The criterion which must be used to decide whether an extraordinary state of the mind is ecstasy, created by the Spiritual Presence, or subjective intoxication is the manifestation of creativity in the former and the lack of it in the latter. The use of this criterion is not without

6. Cited in Jolande Jacobi, *The Psychology of C. G. Jung* (New Haven: Yale University Press, 1943), p. 25.

risk, but it is the only valid criterion the church can employ in "judging the Spirit" (Tillich, 120).

Prophets themselves avow this criterion. "What must be prepared for, and actively experimented with, is the creation of new forms of life" (Daniel Berrigan). Creation is nothing other than the attempt to breathe life again; it is the natural reflection and imitation of an experience with the mystery of life in all its fullness. The prophetic response will not only create, but will support and encourage the creative and prophetic wherever it be (this may distinguish it from false prophecy, which so often is exclusive in its insights—claiming that it should be imitated —or which is jealous of competition from other prophets, as if one's own right to creativity does not also include the desire to encourage others in their creativity). In an age in which history connotes a tomorrow as well as a yesterday, contemplation need not be of things past but also of the future. Thus the act of creation (or seeing in vision the future and giving birth to it) is inherent to contemplation. "God does not think, he creates," Kierkegaard reminds us.

4. Community orientation. We have insisted that the prophetic response is a creative one. But creative of what? Above all of community, or the experience of life and its mysteries—death, evil, rebirth, nature, vocation, the other, love—with others. The first reason why radical prayer is a creation of community is that, as we have seen, prayer takes place at the level of the unconscious, where all persons share symbols and experiences in common. Prayer is then, by reason of its place, radically social. "To pray is to postulate that the reality of others, though independent of me, depends in some degree on the act by which I posit it, that the act contributes in some way to the reality. I am convinced that, in the simplest psychological sense, the thought of others contributes to our make-up." (Marcel, *MJ*, 133) This is why justice becomes a test of the prophet's authenticity because it is the basis of community.

But what community is prayer, as a radical social response to life, meant to create? Here lies the core of the spiritual revolution brought about by the scientific, industrial, and technological revolutions of the last three centuries. For in former times one's "community" was the world in which one lived. At that time, since community was both limited by space (immobile) and by time (too distant and therefore unknown), solitary prayer sufficed as a search by man for God. The only one who could dream of being in touch with everyone was the monk, who touched others throuch ascetic control of his subconscious in prayer and who enjoyed the epitaph: "the monk is one who lives separated from everyone and united to everyone."[7]

But the conquest of space and time in our day, the reduction of the earth to a global village, has drastically altered the condition for social prayer. Community can only mean worldwide community today. Given the possibilities for worldwide brotherhood and knowledge and reduction of enemies of life (especially poverty, disease, and ignorance), to define community primarily as any group less than the whole human race is to "deny the universal"; it is to betray prayer. "Every prophet who denies the universal should be looked on as a false prophet" (Marcel, *MB*, II, 101). Radical community today is the world community. It is to take man as man, not as American, Russian, Chinese, or Frenchman, much less as Protestant, Buddhist, Jew, Catholic. "The progressive sees the Church as a community and the priests as functional within it. I, on the other hand, want to see the only community as that of mankind, and to see the Church as functional within it" (McCabe, 621).

It goes without saying that "community" cannot primarily mean a group that supports and runs an institution, for an institution, even when it is performing a service, is a step removed from prophecy and can only be tolerated by the spirit of prophecy. Community is always a striving for what is not yet;

7. Evagrius of Pontus, *On Prayer*, p. 124.

a presumption that "our group" is already a community is a sure sign that the spirit of prophetic prayer has long since departed from such a grouping. Prayer in such a situation inevitably becomes ritualized and formalized, a look backward rather than an eschatological leap. Community is oriented toward justice, not to what satisfies my personal needs for warmth and kindness. The latter is friendship: "It is here that the 'credibility' of the Church is to be judged, not according to whether it is a community in which we can begin to satisfy our personal need for human warmth and kindness and decent personal relations, but according to whether it is an effective force in the revolutionizing of the world" (McCabe, 625). The word "community," after all, does not come from the word "communion" but from the words *cum* and *munio*, meaning "to build with." The primary meaning of community, then, is a task force bent on building a world of justice among brothers.

That worldwide community is possible is borne witness by a man whose prayerfulness we have referred to elsewhere in discussing his conversion to a psychologically radical response to life. Malcolm X drew his own conclusions from this conversion concerning community—a sign of the authentic prophet he was:

My thinking has been opened up wide in Mecca. In the long letters I wrote to friends, I tried to convey to them my new insights into the American black man's struggle and his problems, as well as the depths of my search for truth and justice. . . . "I've had enough of someone else's propaganda." I'm a human being first and foremost, and as such I'm for whoever and whatever benefits humanity *as a whole* (438).

The sign of community-building is not a new sign with the prophets. Jeremiah's vocation is to all the nations:

> The sound reaches all the inhabitants of the earth,
> to the far ends of the world.
> For Yahweh is indicting the nations,
> arraigning all flesh for judgment (Jer. 25:31).

Jesus, following in the tradition of Judaic prophecy, also emphasized that prophecy was for community. The one prayer he left his followers speaks of *Our* Father: Give *us* this day *our* daily bread; Forgive *us our* trespasses as *we* forgive those who trespass against *us*; Lead *us* not into temptation, but deliver *us* from evil. Jesus invokes groupings of believers, "Where two or three are gathered together in my name, there am I in the midst of them" (Matt. 18:20), and his word is to be spread abroad "to all men," "to the ends of the earth." His teaching on the universal brotherhood of man under the life-giving fatherhood of the Father, whom man addresses intimately as "Abba," becomes a basis for universal love and peace. The early Christian community learned and unlearned with difficulty how the work of the Spirit knows no bounds of race, nationality, or creed, but penetrates "among all the sanctified" (Acts 20:32). This is the way the early Church interpreted the prayer Jesus taught them: "Because there is no solitariness before God (Rom. 14:7f.), there is no prayer which is only 'private prayer,' because each person stands as a member of the church of God."[8]

5. *The price of prophecy*. An ultimate test of the prophet is the price he or she is willing to pay. The prophet is not only called to uprooting injustice to pave the way for the coming of new life, but is also (cf. John the Baptist or Jesus) to suffer the new life in experiencing the death of the old. The new birth of baptism is a birth by fire and destruction. The crucifixion *is* Jesus' baptism and his "consecration," the entering into his glory as mysterious and hidden as that seems to be. To accept death is, for Jesus, the seed for new life: "Unless the grain of wheat first die. . . ."

This price that the prophet continually pays is not a self-induced suffering. There is no masochistic pleasure in it, no enjoyment of suffering for its own sake. It is the direct result of

8. W. Hillman, "Das Gebet im Neuen Testamentum," *LfTuK* (IV), p. 541.

angering powers and principalities and of preaching the Good News that is truly News: that the poor and outcasts are persons. Those who find that suffering and even death are not a threat from others in their lives may generally presume that they have forsaken their prophetic vocation. Just as cynicism is the price one pays for having had high ideals and empty results, so security is the fill for a person once called to prophecy. Only an understanding of life as comfortable and secure can ignore the sufferings that are real to those who preach the Gospel and who undergo the conversion to becoming a brother that beckons every son and daughter of man. This is why one's understanding of evil and suffering is almost a test of one's capacity to respond to life as a mystery and not merely as a problem. For those who experience life as mystery, the only real loss is to have lived without surrendering oneself. "What does it profit a man if he gain the whole world but suffer the loss of his soul?"

To pay a price for one's passion for life is itself to be creative. The prophet's suffering is creative within himself so that loss of a loved one or of some other mystery in life (e.g. freedom) makes one treasure life all the more; that is, it radicalizes him, touching his very roots. How history has been altered by the deaths of Jesus; of Lenin's brother; of John Kennedy; of Martin Luther King, Jr.; or the sickness of Ignatius of Loyola or Francis of Assisi; or the imprisonment of a Malcolm X, an Eldridge Cleaver, a John of the Cross or the Berrigans. Prophetic suffering is always a creative suffering.

From time to time, the prophet's sole sustaining power may be hope—which, of course, is not optimism, but the capacity to sustain one's belief that life is a gift when all else seems to dictate otherwise. Hope means that the power to deal with evil powers is greater than oneself and must ultimately triumph, that "the gates of hell shall not prevail."

Those who respond by throwing themselves into battling life's enemies are responding to life radically. They are prayerful people. Human history, and in particular that moment in it

which is the society into which they hurl themselves, will never
be the same again. Running from our prophetic vocation, or
covering it up on the other hand—and for whatever reason at
all—means everything is lost. Life is missed for it is never
shared, never handed on to others. Even our desire to personally enjoy life becomes tragic and a selfish failure, for no one in
the end enjoys life alone. "There is such a thing as losing one's
soul," warns Hocking, "and that is rejecting one's call to
prophecy" (513).

CHAPTER 6

Developing Our Capacities for Mysticism and Prophecy

The first seed of the longing for Justice
blows through the soul like the wind.
The taste for good will plays in it like a breeze.
The consummation of this seed
is a greening of the soul
that is like that
of the ripening world.
Now the soul honors God
by the doing of just deeds.
The soul is only as strong as its works.[1]
—Hildegard of Bingen

1. Gabriele Uhlein, trans., *Meditations with Hildegard of Bingen* (Sante Fe: Bear & Co., 1982), 123.

If prayer is our radical response to life, our initial question—
How do we become prayerful people?—may be simply put
now: How do we become people who respond radically to life?
In particular, since learning to pray means learning to root
oneself into life through that topsoil which is one's culture, how
do we Americans, in this time in history, become radical responders to life and its mysteries? How is this radical response
brought about in our culture and how shall we seek out these
opportunities to make the best use of them?

EXPERIENCE OF LIFE

One learns life by living it. As recognizable a truism as this
appears to be, it is too seldom advanced by writers on prayer
who seem so often to be intent on moralizing about life rather
than encouraging the living of it. But morality is only a small
part of life's problems. It barely touches life's mysteries, the
area of prayer, at all. This experience of life was the "wisdom"
that was the achievement of wise men of more simple cultures:
they had lived life, known it from experience, and therefore
were sages on its fortunes and its fates. Real life really lived is
the only avenue for learning about prayer.

The reason why older persons in principle have much to pass
on to others about prayer is not (as our spiritual Platonists would
suggest) because their faculties for distraction have slowed
down or that they are less passionate. It is because, in theory,
they have lived longer; they have experienced more of life. To
the extent that this is a myth and that they have not experienced more of life's mysteries (perhaps having been exces-
sively taken up in its problems), they forfeit this spiritual
charisma that younger generations might hope to profit from.
But when a seventy-year-old has lived life with heart and eyes
open, there is no greater charisma and no more genuine youth-
fulness than his or her wisdom encapsulated in a twinkling eye,
a lively parable, a tolerant heart, or an encouraging word.

The process of becoming a prayerful people is the process of developing our capacities for responding to life radically—of developing our powers of mysticism (enjoying life) and of prophecy (struggling to share it). Any attempts to develop these capacities can rightly contribute to our spiritual development and we treat here in skeletal outline some such efforts in American culture.

DEVELOPING OUR CAPACITIES FOR MYSTICISM

On Becoming Aware Recollection, or meditation, can be for us an exercise in becoming aware. Marcel suggests that we recollect when we realize we are "at the mercy of life and without a hold upon it" *(PE,* 23 f.). Meditation is a getting hold of my relation to life: it is a recollection on life and its mysteries. First we admit the existence of these mysteries and then we recollect, turn back (or turn forward) on our relationship to them. These recollections become the rudder to our attitudes, the steering given our response to life.

When we meditate we choose a topic and spend some time alone with it (we may be considering the topic with others or by ourselves), concentrating on it to some depth. The stuff we meditate on is the mysteries of life. A meditation is an examination of our roots. An example of a profitable meditation on suffering and evil might be to consider and thereby become aware of the following situations existing in one's own land: Slip for a moment into the soul of a black girl whose womanhood is blighted not because she is ugly, but because she is black and by definition all blacks are ugly. "Imagine how an impoverished mother feels as she watches the light of creativity snuffed out in her children by schools which dull the mind and environments which rot the soul" (Grier, 210). Imagine yourself as a parent of a soldier killed in Vietnam. For what?

To allow these meditations to touch us and to affect our

awareness and then our attitudes and our actions is to become prayerful. It is clear from these examples of the mystery of evil and suffering, which are not at all distant from us, that the newspaper, news magazines, and other media offer daily chances for becoming aware. One is reminded of the woman who was reading a newspaper in a dark church and was approached by the priest. "This is no place to read the newspaper," said he. "But I'm suffering with these people in the paper," she replied.

Since the sixteenth century, meditation has come to mean an isolated and independent activity in itself. Yet the age-old Christian monastic tradition took meditation as an intermediary function between the experience of *lectio*, hearing the word of God, and *oratio*, speaking to God in response to this hearing. A consequence of atomizing and isolating meditation has been the inability of modern man to contemplate, to synthesize what his life is all about. The examples for meditation we have offered above call for a reinstatement of meditation as an intermediary function: as a bridge between understanding and acting. We can no longer afford the luxury, either as a people or as individuals, of meditation being an act in itself, a private discipline. The richest monastic tradition is that meditation is meant to serve by providing a synthetic factor in our daily living. Thus meditation was said to fulfill itself in contemplation or a wholistic experience of our life's activities and attitudes so that "the love of neighbor which animates man is no longer an apostolate 'for the love of God' but is the embracing of the world where God is everything in everyone."[2]

It stands to reason that meditation can be of things future as much as of things past. Reading *Future Shock* initiates for many the sense that history means tomorrow as much as yesterday. Meditating on the future is no luxury today; it is an indispensi-

2. R. Javelet, "Psychologie des auteurs spirituels du XII siècle," *Revue Science Religieuse* (1959): 265.

ble activity that must precede our building a future. One idea for the future, worthy of our time and meditation, would be the following adage: "No man is good enough to be another man's master." What might be the consequences of such a principle put into practice? How do I put it into practice in my life, in my culture? How do we initiate it in our lives and world?

The process of becoming aware often reaches a high point in friendship, where one learns of the worth and the price of life's mysteries: we are supported in what we experience when we share it, and we learn from others' lives when we encourage them to share their responses with us. Friendship is our sharing deeply with others as equals, and it is in this sharing that many today will say that they experience their deepest moments of prayer. Frankie, in Theodore Rubin's novel *Coming Out*, offers his understanding of friendship "If you feel for somebody, if something happens between you—deep down where it counts —then things can start moving—sometimes in another direction. Things can change. People can change. . . . We will never be the same again. Is this really what love is—a state of change?" From friendship and within comes the awareness that precedes conversion.

All love is not being in love. Friendships are possible for those who will risk them among enemies; that is, among those one fears. It is from those most different from us that we often learn the most, which is just one reason why travel—and in particular living in a culture different from one's own and learning the language of that culture—is one of the most powerful of awareness experiences. Traveling, because it uproots a person from his own way of seeing life through his own culture, assures a new awareness of the culture temporarily left behind at the same time that it invites him to embrace life lived differently; i.e., in a new cultural setting. By travel I do not mean hobnobbing from one Hilton Hotel to another or isolating oneself while abroad, as so many Americans do (I overheard the remark from one American tourist in a Parisian café: "Look! They have bread too!"). I mean actually entering other cultures, becoming vulnerable to them. Now, when persons under twenty-eight can fly to Europe and back for less than $200, a young person dedicated to prayer would need a solid excuse not to earn his way to leave his culture and open himself or herself to other worlds. The young man who complains that a year off from his university will delay his getting a job is only revealing his priorities: life is secondary to career for such a person. Of course, foreign subcultures are also available within our country's boundaries, though often the tensions involved in entering ghettos different from our own make a visit to another continent preferable from the point of view of becoming aware.

One becomes aware of life's mysteries by inserting oneself into nature, becoming vulnerable once again to the place of our own origins. Camping and excursions into countrysides and seacoasts offer opportunities for many families to reexperience their spiritual roots, as we indicated in the first chapter. In addition, man's own artifacts, beginning with the dynamism of fire (who has not gazed and recollected before a crackling fire?) and including his balloons and his candles, his gliders and his planes, his ships and his bridges, should not be scorned as "inferior" subjects for meditation. They, too, beckon us to a mystery that we know, from understanding nature as a mystery, takes us out of ourselves.

Life is at many crucial junctures a question of chance. Perhaps a chance exposure to poliomyelitis puts someone in the hospital at a critical moment in his life, forcing reflection and recollection on him; perhaps the sudden death of a friend; perhaps the loss of a friend; perhaps a chance encounter with a stranger; perhaps an unexpected article or book we read, a movie we see, a record we hear. Who can predict or catalog such critical occurrences? Yet who can ignore them or cut them out from the process of our becoming aware of life and its mysteries.

An obvious question to ask that will enrich our meditation is simply: Where and when, under what circumstances, do we meditate the best? In seeking out these occasions one is caring about meditation.

Since psychological response to life of a radical kind is itself a process in becoming honest, one can inquire of the contemporary means of letting oneself grow in honesty. Most prominent among them is, no doubt, processes of psychotherapy and its variations: group dynamics, sensitivity seminars, T-groups, and others. Any or all of these commitments (for that is what they demand) can be a most powerful experience of radical change and awareness resulting in authentic experiences of metanoia or conversion and ushering in levels of insight and new plateaus of psychological existence. For many persons authentic prayer —radical attitudes toward life—are derived from them. Specialists trained to handle these sessions will acknowledge that not everyone has the temperament to undergo these "trials" and that some sessions are more adapted to certain persons' needs than others. The reservations I hold on these means to prayer are as follows: That such experiences are themselves *stages* of one's spiritual (that is, life) growth and therefore are to be flung away and not clung to. "The encounter group is not life, nor is it a viable substitute for it, but it can be an aid to more effective living."[3] Secondly, that these experiences will find their fulfillment in social conversion as does all authentic conversion to love. The psychological can never replace the social, and is so often dependent to a greater degree on the social than many "psychological converts" seem to be aware. These important points established, we can still say that sound psychotherapeutic sessions can achieve great honesty for an individual and thus great growth in prayer.

One grows in honesty, as we indicated in Chapter 4, by growing in appreciation of oneself. For this it is often necessary to

3. Gerard Egan, *Encounter: Group Processes for Interpersonal Growth* (Belmont, Calif.: Brooks, Cole Co., 1970), p. iii.

test oneself, to exert oneself in new directions, to challenge oneself or put onself where he or she will be challenged. If honesty also means growing into awareness of what one lacks, then education and reeducation and rereeducation is necessary daily fare for the prayerful person: reading, savoring the arts (as opposed to strutting them), evaluating one's travel and one's daily encounters with others, attending lectures and inserting oneself into places where thinking is going on. All these become means to honest responses to existence, as do admitting one's limitations (so often built into one's greatest gifts or skills) to one's family, to one's community, and to oneself. With this honesty comes a new willingness to express oneself, whether that be by learning to cook (or eat) interesting foods, making ceramics, painting, listening to or writing music, writing poetry, learning film history: our willingness to indulge interests we have by going back to school or pursuing them in some personal way is the giving birth to our creativity.

Letting Go Prayer means not only being aware, but giving oneself over to one's vision. One does not teach another person freedom; only the value of pursuing it can be rightly passed on. For the pursuit of freedom is the most personal task we engage ourselves in. Yet one aspect of the pursuit of freedom is the capacity to relax, to receive, and in current America there seems to be two methods especially popular for "letting oneself go" or "loosening up": drugs and drink.

1. Drugs.
I recall a twenty-five-year-old Dutchman, whose black beard and flower in his jeans pocket breathed something of the blithe and free spirit he was, if he used drugs. "Why should I?" he exclaimed. "I get high on music and prayer." Hundreds of thousands of other youths do not share his experience. What can one say about authentic prayer and drugs? First, to dispose of the obvious ethical question (which, unfortunately, is very often all that religious writers will touch on when dealing with this sub-

ject): we do not mean excess use of drugs or commitment to dangerous drugs. We are presuming an intelligent use of drugs, for excesses in any area are not to be the norm for asking the question: Can we be served by them? Can we grow through them? Secondly, granting some "safe" control (preferably self-control) of the choice and use of drugs, there seems to be no question that drugs can aid in two important areas of prayer: that of awareness of the beauties in the world around one— colors, sounds, people, nature itself seen "bathed in a new light" —to say nothing of simply the advantages in leaving behind the everyday world of rational worry and fret in temporary withdrawal. Nor, for anyone who has taken such trips, is the argument that they are "egocentric" forceful. They are less egocentric than the retreat of former spiritual days when an individual could be completely noninteracting and noncommunicating with his fellow retreatants. The taking of drugs is, at least at a secondary level, a very communal experience: the passing of a hashish pipe, the sharing of the same marijuana joint. (It is a little exercise in getting over one's overly middle-class hangups regarding hygiene.) The atmosphere created by pot, no less than the atmosphere created by incense in Byzantine or former Roman Catholic services, is conducive to "communing" in a mystical sense.

It is also clear that drugs properly taken can aid one in appreciation, for nothing is so spontaneous as a "thank you" once one has experienced a new awareness. One's capacity to appreciate grows when one's awareness has been opened up in some way. We can say then that drugs definitely can aid in becoming a prayerful people, provided, of course, that they are wisely administered and understood. (All spiritual traditions speak of the need for wise counsel when embarking on a spiritual journey, which is always a dangerous voyage: there is no reason why such counsel is less needed in the matter of drugs today.)

But to say that drugs can aid prayer is not saying that they fulfill all the requirements for authentic prayer. In particular, I see two reservations of a substantial kind for allowing drugs too influential a place in one's prayer life. The first is that a drug experience is exactly that—an experience. And the essence of prayer, as we have demonstrated, is not an ecstatic experience. Hagiographers, so prolific in number and words, who have piously reported the extraordinary in prayerful persons' lives, can take much credit for the excesses incurred by drug-takers seeking spiritual trips today. The essence of prayer, as we have frequently alluded to in this book, is change of heart, metanoia, conversion. Change to what? To becoming a radical lover. But a radical lover is a lover by deeds as well as by feelings or words; he is a man or woman for others, not just for his own mystical experiences.

The second difficulty with drugs as a center of one's spirituality is related: that is, the prophecy—work for the right to life of others—with its creativity in building community, is a fruit of one's conversion. Can a drug-user also contribute to justice on earth? If not, he or she is less humane than the most reclusive hermit of the past who at least in theory (and probably through ESP) was contributing to society's well-being. Braden warns, "There are now many more quietists than activists within the drug movement as a whole, and the problem grows more pressing with every day that passes."[4] He would seem to answer our question pessimistically. Furthermore, the obvious burgeoning of criminal elements in the sale and pushing of drugs in America today does not augur well for the future of the "pure" users who desire it for spiritual purposes. For the big business of drugs is increasing, not decreasing, economic injustices in this country, contributing to the wealth of the already (criminally) wealthy. How much of this criminal element in the drug trade is, like the bootlegging of Prohibition days, the result of scrupu-

4. William Braden, *The Private Sea: LSD & the Search for God* (Chicago: Quadrangle Books, 1967), pp. 214f.

lous laws will be seen only after drug legislation is brought up to date.

We conclude that drugs may be a stage in one's prayer life but no more. A radical response to life is meant to be as big as life, and therefore bigger than any chemicals. Yet to call drug-taking a stage personally and historically for spirituality is not to say nothing on drugs' behalf. For drugs can democratize spirituality, which has for so long been imagined to be in the hands and hearts of the wealthy, leisurely classes. "Now the common man can share the mystical visions of the saints themselves, and it is no longer necessary to spend ten or twenty years in a Zen monastery to achieve true *satori*" (Braden, 119). The depths of the human consciousness and unconsciousness are being explored by modern adventurers. (It is worth noting that William James, who confessed he was "constitutionally" shut out from mystical experience, still was opened up to an "entirely different form of consciousness" on taking drugs).

2. Drink.

William James made an observation years ago that seems to have gone little explored: "The sway of alcohol over mankind is unquestionably due to its power to stimulate the mystical faculties of human nature, usually crushed to earth by the cold facts and dry criticisms of the sober hours. Sobriety diminishes, discriminates and says 'no'; drunkenness expands, unites, and says 'yes'. . . . To the poor and the unlettered it stands in the place of symphony concerts and of literature; and it is part of the deeper mystery and tragedy of life" (James, 297). In this passage James asserts that there exists such a psychical reality as "the mystical faculties" and that these faculties are the Yes and expansion-producing elements of man's psyche. More than that, he asserts that there is a correlation between material poverty and "spiritual" poverty, between the way a person seeks to assert his psychological response to life and the access his culture allows him to these means. One cannot be radical psychologically and not radical socially unless he is still *in via*.

No doubt it is the experience of many that a good party, drink included, is a marvelous form of recuperation, of relaxation and letting go. So it is. And there is no a priori reason to be overly suspect of the role drink plays in letting us be spontaneous, passionate, and honest. A party is as good a place for prayer as any other place, possibly because the odds for persons being present as equals in communication is greater due to the party spirit, it is better than most places.

Reservations regarding the role of drink are no different from those regarding drugs. The need for drug-drink, as James indicates in the passage above, testifies to the great "unused" faculty: the human capacity for mysticism or radical psychological change. When a culture and its religion fail to encourage this capacity, people turn to alternate stimulants. Perhaps the greatest human waste dissipated by a culture that does not alleviate the burdens of the poor is the spiritual potential of both rich and poor that is so seldom allowed to bear fruit. The thriving businesses of our familiar bars and taverns are testimony that no mystique of mysticism needs to be cultivated: mysticism is already acknowledged. It is prophecy that needs recognition, for the griping and bitching that goes on at the bar rail (cf. Joe in the movie *Joe*) is pseudoprophecy; an escape from the personal demands of authentic prophecy.

Yoga, Zen, or physical disciplines of some more personalized kind, as well as sensitivity sessions (for certain persons only), suggest themselves as suitable methods for learning the kind of relaxation and letting go that prayer presumes. Above all, one only learns letting go by trying it and trusting the company and the situation one is in. If our experience of awareness is real and powerful enough, it draws us out of ourselves *(ecstacy)*, beyond our self-doubts and inhibitions. Lively celebrations of a communal kind ideally accomplish this.

Conversion What means does our culture offer for the conversion experience? We detect at least three basic ways by which one may reach a stage of radical change of self: place and manner of living, study and acquisition of skills, Pentecostalism.

1. Place and manner of living.

Were it not so overwhelming an influence on our attitude toward life, one would think we could talk of prayer without talking of where one lives. But one's life-response takes place, like all our responses, in relation to our experience of life about us: and that experience is the world we live in. The mobility that has come to characterize American society indicates a fundamental revolution that has taken place in the past fifty years: Today one chooses (granted, the choice is often predetermined in great part by available jobs, friends, family) where he or she will set up home.

This is (or can be) in itself a major spiritual breakthrough, because to live in a "new" place, outside one's own cultural region, is to put oneself in a proximate position of conversion, of being changed. This is evident from the following examples: A black man choosing to leave his southern farm and move to Chicago is, within at least three years in that city, a different person: he becomes as a rule angry and demanding of his rights. There is the example of Pope John XXIII. What is it that made this Italian so fundamentally different (a radical difference that others, especially nonbelievers, could sense by insight in communicating with him) from all the other Italian popes of this century? Surely one important aspect was his nonaristocratic heritage; but another, perhaps equally important, was his living outside a Roman ecclesiastical culture for several years as a minority (i.e., a newcomer) in a Turkish (Moslem) culture. Another example of conversion by place of residence is George Orwell, that recognized prophet of mining England, who chose to live outside a writer's milieu and in the miner's world: working as a miner, living as one, and writing in his shack by gaslight

in the evenings. His choice shortened his life but in turn gave
life to miners; he insisted he would have it no other way. One
is reminded of Paul's advice, so little followed within church
circles of do-gooders: "never be condescending, but make real
friends with the poor" (Rom. 12:16). Suffering and exposure
seem to be the key to conversion. And *where* one chooses to live
can provide such an exposure, or can forever cut it off.

The question of where one lives implies also that of *how* one
lives. Relatively new kinds of life-styles are burgeoning everywhere in western countries today, as the media are more and
more eager to report. Role switching in marriages; voluntary
family councils to eliminate the family car, or to determine a
modest budget on which the whole family can live in order to
render working hours less prominence than hours for
creativity; changing jobs simply because one is not happy at
one's work; parents expressing their feelings, doubts, and fears
and holding conversations (instead of lectures) with one's teenaged children realizing that they can teach us: Who can predict
the possible rerooting and uprooting that are the spiritual benefits of these efforts at conversion? In addition we witness a
growing experiment at community living. These radical communities are symptomatic of the deeply felt need for a new
intimacy, a new attitude toward relationships that lie at the
heart of authentic prayer conversion. Those who venture into
them risk much in doing so, especially at the early and more
experimental stages, and in this sense become reluctant prophets for the rest of us. Mistakes or extremes may be part and
parcel of these early stages of experimentation but the message
remains: until we change our life-style we may never touch our
prayer. Today persons of immense caliber and depth and experience are being attracted to these groupings. One can only
hope that from these experiments a life may flourish that is
profoundly turned to personal and social conversion. Only a
Platonic bias that what is good must last eternally would judge
a communitarian experiment on the basis of how long it lasts.

The more spiritual criterion would be: what roots did it uncover; what depths did it plummet?

2. Study and the acquisition of skills.

William James distinguishes two kinds of conversion: the first is volitional or one built up with critical points over a period. This kind of conversion is much less a sudden experience than it is an art acquired by determination and dedication. The story of Ralph Nader is proof in itself; his effectiveness is due to his expertise as a trained and proficient lawyer (which also aids in attracting equally competent investigators to work with him). Where would Nader's raids have carried him without his skills won by hard study as a lawyer?

We have in the example of Nader a key to adult conversion experience: that profound change is won very often by struggle and dedication, not by instantaneous moments of enlightenment. Moreover, we have here the basis for a bona fide and effective understanding of vocation from a theological perspective: We are all called to a single vocation—that of building up life, in ourselves and for others. Whether the particular enactment of that vocation be by way of our parenthood (putting the mystery of each child first and presenting life first before each child as a mystery) or our profession (using law to create justice among men such as Nader does, not to stifle it for our profit), or by both is less significant than that we respond to that primary vocation by being readily converted and reconverted toward its demands on us and our time. The surest spiritual weapon of the professional person is his profession: law, medicine, business, politics; when they are self-critical and employed for the sake of rooting life and uprooting death-forces they have no parallel for inciting metanoia.

3. Pentecostalism.

The second type of conversion experience of which James speaks is a surrender of one's will. The growth of Pentecostalism in America's middle class indicates the spiritual void and vacuity of lives there. Interestingly, a great percentage of persons attracted to Pentecostalism are persons for whom wrestling with the evil spirit called loneliness has been particularly acute. But Pentecostalism's appeal goes deeper than this, for it clearly performs the function of conversion: its converts speak of a "deeper awareness" of reality and life about them as a result of their experience. These positive contributions of Pentecostalism cannot be denied and adherents will allow no one to diminish them.

But there are fundamental ingredients of authentic prayer as we have outlined it that much Pentecostalism seems incapable of providing and that therefore indicate that Pentecostalism might be only a stage in one's spiritual journey. The first is that conversion (like spiritual experience) is not an end in itself: the changed person (changed into a lover) is the goal. Does Pentecostalism provide an actual change of heart deep enough that the convert goes out to others in an act of love (as opposed to an act of proselytizing) that is based on social justice? How much room is there in Pentecostalism for social prophecy? To the extent that there is not, to that degree Pentecostalism is only a stage of one's prayer experience. Historically, Pentecostals seem notoriously poor at providing services for others, for witnessing to prophetic needs. So much emotion (and emotional conversion is not ipso facto radical conversion) is spent on their type of psychological experience that one can wonder what energy is left for others. Nor is this an idle academic criticism. We all are aware that much of the black man's religion in America was Pentecostal until the advent of Black Power. Is it mere coincidence that when a black prophetic movement appeared on the scene, the former psychological religion faded into the background? Does this not point to a basic incompatibility, or at least to an incapacity of Pentecostal prayer to meet the rigorous demands of sacrificial prophetic prayer? Nor is it convincing to argue that Pentecostalism prepared the black man for his coming to power (for one can just as convincingly argue that it aided the whites in keeping the nigger down and content, his emotions dissipated on private soul-saving). Perhaps one meaning of Pentecostalism's great inroads into whiter middle-class America is that that class is as oppressed and enchained today as was black America for two centuries.

Certain sects of Pentecostalism exhibit an anti-intellectualism, a frequent iconoclasm, and a dogmatism—"revivalism has always assumed that only its own type of religious experience can be perfect" (James, 185). Such sects eliminate themselves as any lasting spiritual way. Yet Pentecostalism's consistent anti-rationalism is well received by persons of newly oppressed classes in our society today. To be able to marry some of its fervor and psychological dedication with prophetic needs may be a viable contribution it could well make in America. But any prayer built on conversion must heed James' observation that conversion is "in its essence a normal adolescent phenomenon" (164). It is a characteristic of an adult that he need not dwell on his (or another's) conversion but grows up to root and uproot, destroy and create. One looks for social criticism and creation among our praying Pentecostals.

Appreciation of Life Appreciation is not an acquired virtue but a response that is spontaneous if it is anything. Yet there is an element of appreciation that can at least be *re*learned, especially in a culture where gifts are usually considered of value according to their dollar estimate. The process of becoming appreciative derives in particular from the young, and especially from children who have, because life is not long enough yet to have bored them, maintained a gratefulness at just being alive and meeting life's beauties for the first time. Some would ascribe a child's contribution in this regard to his inner capacity to receive spontaneously. 'Amen I tell you, whoever does not receive the Kingdom of God as a little child, shall not enter therein" (Mark 10:15).

The child teaches adults the art of receiving, which reaches a high point in the act of amazement. When the problems of life so stifle its mysteries that nothing any longer amazes us, we are no longer capable of responding radically to life. Only this invitation to wonder will move us to enjoy ourselves. A child is not afraid to live in his imagination and play because his imagination is no more "his own possession" than is life itself. Thus there lies an important link between thankfulness and play. Only the thankful person can play and the playful person is the best subject to pray.

While we suggest that an adult may learn much about becoming a prayerful person from children, we repeat the point emphasized in Chapter 1: that a child cannot pray as such. It should be evident by now why this is so: because a child cannot respond to life's mysteries. "To live life to the end is not a childish task," notes Pasternak. The adult who can happily entertain the child in himself welcomes it in others in spite of culture's pressures to play an adult role is a prayerful person. Psychologist Gordon Allport emphasizes that a child is deprived of contemplation: "To feel oneself meaningfully linked to the whole of Being is not possible before puberty."[5] Portnoy explains that the reason why youthful musical prodigies are technicians but not creators is that "one must first have endured life's experiences before he has something to write about."[6] Still, if prayer is response to life, then all efforts to introduce children to life (for example, education, answering of questions, positing of questions and distinctions, revelation of life's problems) can also be efforts to introduce them to prayer. This learning will mark the passage from childhood to adolescence. The ultimate point of departure from adolescence to adulthood is, of course, one's response to evil and one's awareness that he or she has a vocation; that is, that he is capable of doing something about life's

5. Gordon Allport, *Becoming* (New Haven: Yale Univ. Press, 1955), p. 94.

6. Julius Portnoy, *Music in the Life of Man* (New York: Holt, Rinehart and Winston, 1963), p. 42.

enemies. At this stage in life one can or cannot become a prayerful person, but not before. For an adult manifests appreciation by sharing.

DEVELOPING OUR CAPACITIES FOR PROPHECY

It is one thing to develop our powers of saying "yes" to life, of enjoying it, of deepening our awareness and appreciation of it, of rendering ourselves honest in face of it and open to a deeper conversion by it. But it is another art, and a much neglected one, to develop our capacities to say "no" to the enemies of life, the death-elements in our culture. A positivist philosophy (so much a part of the American cultural scene) combined with a sanctification of obedience (so much a part of the Roman ecclesiastical scene since the sixteenth century—"to obey is to do God's will"—a rare understanding of Providence if ever there was one) and a parading of piety (so much a part of Protestant piety, as if White House prayer services were necessarily as pleasing to God as they are to politicians' fortunes) have consorted to convince us to feel compunction when raising a negative voice. There is no evidence that Jesus felt guilt at driving money-changers out of the Temple or at berating the hypocrisy of the guardians of the Jewish theocracy. The power of saying "no" is very often the power of the Spirit. Before one plants, one turns over the soil.

Associating with Prophets The art of uprooting is best learned from others more expert than ourselves. The most effective way of learning the art of prophecy is to actually live with persons who have developed these powers: to work with them, to discuss with them, to observe them in action and reaction, in victory and in defeat. This would require, very often, our going out of our way, perhaps out of our life-style for awhile. But it is difficult to imagine time better invested, no matter for how short a period.

A second though less effective way of associating with prophets is to visit them, to listen to them. Perhaps this means watching keenly for the occasions they will visit our city or our area; perhaps it means inviting them to some institution of which we are a part; perhaps it means corresponding with them or writing to them inviting ourselves to their place of residence for a weekend; perhaps it means visiting them in jail.

Another way of associating with prophets is to read what they have done, said, or written, and then to reflect on its meaning for our particular situation (a worthy subject for meditation). The willingness to read and to study the life and work of a prophet has obvious application to our relationship to deceased prophets. How about the life of a George Orwell or a Mahatma Gandhi or a Camilo Torres?; or a Cesar Chavez or a Daniel Berrigan?; or the insights and the self-sacrifice of a Karl Marx? What *are* the consequences, for example, of Marx's remarks that "the more these conscious illusions of the ruling classes are shown to be false and the less they satisfy common sense, the more dogmatically they are asserted and the more deceitful, moralizing and spiritual becomes the language of established society." What food for thought—and conversion—are these words for Americans, swamped as we are with daily pieties, but so little policies, from our politicians.

One reason that association with prophets is so essential for our developing our prophetic vocation is that I can conceive of no other means for developing courage other than associating with persons more courageous than myself. Courage is like tennis: one develops in it by being challenged by those more experienced than oneself.

Investigating the Enemies of Life To be adult means to possess the knowledge of when to say Yes and when to say No. What good is education if it fails to instruct us in what to say No to? And in how to say this No effectively? An indispensable means of developing prophetically is constantly putting the question:

Where are the evil spirits, those that interfere with life as a gift, in my culture at this time?

Evil spirits such as the ones we enumerated in the previous chapter do not wander about the land disembodied. They are cunning and smart and know that the best place to prolong their existence and to implement their powers is in institutions. An institution is a home for evil spirits just as a dog's fur is a home for the tick and the flea. No institution (it is, after all, man-created) is immune from this rule. Thus the Protestant principle that the need for continual institutional criticism and reform is a prayer itself applies to every institution. With good reason persons might begin with criticism of the churches, especially those who claim to be "radical" and believer at the same time. (Have we not maintained that to be radical is to be self-critical, and critical of one's own situation first of all?) When a culture or its institutions no longer serve life and pass it on but rather usurp to themselves the priority life deserves, then prophetic pray must call the culture or its institutions to account.

The Corporate Information Center, a research agency recently set up by the National Council of Churches to investigate church institutions, has uncovered these facts: American churches, while criticizing the Vietnam involvement verbally, reap great benefits from it—$6.2 million in 1970 alone from their investment in prime military contractors. Such information is just a baby step in uncovering the complicity of church institutions and death forces; one still looks for a comparable research agency in the Roman Catholic Church's investments. Is the Catholic believer so indifferent that he does not love his church enough to criticize it? Then let him love life enough to criticize the churches to the extent that they obstruct life's mysteries! There is something unconvincing about believers who make their way to Congress by saying No to their government's immoral war but never say No to their church's silence and complicity in that same war.

Surely, beyond opulent ecclesiastical institutions there are numerous others that need profound and considered criticism: "defense" departments; "educational" institutions; "justice" departments and court systems; entertainment institutions; news and press institutions; prisons; business and banking establishments; hospitals; old age homes; unions and professional associations: Are these creations of man serving human life or manipulating life in order that they be served?[7] Hard questions need to be put to our institutions which make such loud and public claims to serving us: How much thinking goes on in our educational institutions? How much prayerfulness is developed in our church and affiliated institutions? How much rehabilitation is accomplished in our prisons? How much protection is given the weak in our judicial system? How many necessary goods (as opposed to luxurious ones) are manufactured by our industry and promoted by our advertising enterprises? There is history to study: How were like evils combated in the past? There are laboratories (cf. Alinsky's or Illich's) in which research and experimentation in facing down these evils may be developed along with a criterion for evaluating one's efforts. There are alternative institutions to support and develop (the so-called underground press, for example).

Stepping Back to Relearn Outrage and Love Proper consideration of one's prophetic vocation may well demand a temporary withdrawal, a stepping back for a better and freer vision, from institutions or cultures of which we are a part. If we are truly interested in developing our prophetic powers, then this freedom to step back is not a luxury but a necessity. A prophetic call is a deep one within us and it demands some time and space for itself—not only to recollect, to get perspective, but also to breathe freshly in order that alternatives might be born anew.

7. My *Religion USA: An Inquiry into Religion and Culture by way of TIME Magazine* (Dubuque: Listening Press, 1971) attempts to do this with a particularly influential publication and offers a method that is adaptable to other publications.

This decision to step back is often itself a prophetic No to the status quo such as we find so frequently in the lives of prophets. Consider John the Baptist, for example, who divorced himself from regular religious expressions despite the fact that he was probably of a priestly family. The New that the prophet announces often requires its own gestation period and place free from the old.

We must develop our capacity for outrage and adult anger, it appears, from purifying our love. For the relation of love and anger is inextricable. Anger is as sure a signal of love as smoke is of fire. Where one's capacity to become outraged at injustices is smothered and barely smolders, so does one's capacity for loving justice. It follows then that the development of the prophet in each of us waits for the development of the mystic in each of us. With growth in our powers to love life will advance our urge to share it and to wrestle with its enemies. Adult anger is not buckshot anger, exploding in every direction at slight provocations. It is finely aimed and honed anger arising from a care for the beloved, not from an overly sensitive or hot-headed reaction to inconveniences. One's care for life fully lived can surely hone one's capacity for anger so that it finds a productive and creative channel in which to accomplish its work, which is a great work: facing down life's demonic and powerful evil spirits and principalities. To develop in love of life, to enjoy it more fully, to allow our mysticism its rightful preeminence *is* to develop as a prophet too.

In calling once again for a place for the ethical and the prophetic in a Christian prayer life, we are advocating the only firm foundation for a new spirituality, that of reflection and consequent action regarding justice (our suffering brother) and society (the forces that impose injustice). For the Judeo-Christian God, Yahweh, is a God of justice. This spirituality replaces that kind which we have all endured long enough, that based on "God and me." In this new spirituality there can be no substitute (not even enthusiasm is a proper substitute) for professional skills and learning. Proper uprooting, no less than authentic rerooting, demands the best the human person and persons in society can procure. It requires excellence.

THE ARTIST AS A SPIRITUAL GURU

A valuable question to ask for a people bent on being prayerful is who are the people, and where are they, who radically respond to life? Who can reveal our roots to us? In cultures where all of creation is honored for its sacredness and not just a sacralized religious piece of it, the artist's is before most others' the soul thirsty for life. "Art," observes Santayana, is "more spiritual than dogma." The poets, the painters, the musicians, the script writers—these are frequently those who lead the struggle with the demons of life in our day. The artist calls up our common roots so that we all might examine, enjoy, and criticize them. Artists are the "monks" of a lay culture, not asking to be imitated in life-style or morality (cf. Tolstoy: "The poet skims off the best of life and puts it in his work. That is why his work is beautiful and his life bad"), but of inviting others to plummet their recognition of the spiritual, of life. The artist is a listener to life: he responds in his poetry or his painting or his music to what life has done to him. He is unusually sensitive to certain aspects of life, often with extraordinary powers of concentration and recall, (one recalls how Hemingway was capable of being engaged in a lively conversation at a party and still listen in on another at the other end of the room).

Plato explained the artist's special quest for roots by his being empowered with a divine mandate; Aristotle had a more secular interpretation for the artist's sensitivity: "There was never a great genius without a tincture of madness." An artist is sensitive to life because he is open to contemplation, or an experience of the whole. "All art exists to communicate states of consciousness which are higher synthetic wholes than those of ordinary experience."[8] Tolstoy pronounces on his vocation:

An artist's mission must not be to produce an irrefutable solution to a problem, but to compel us to love life in all its countless and inexhaustible manifestations. If I were told I might write a book in which I should demonstrate beyond any doubt the correctness of my opinions on every social problem I should not waste two hours at it; but if I were told that what I wrote would be read twenty years from now by people who are children today and that they would read and laugh over my book and love life more because of it, then I should devote all my life and strength to such a work.[9]

How many adolescents have first encountered the depths and tragedy of human existence on reading *Romeo and Juliet* or seeing it played on stage or screen? Or on reading *War and Peace* experience the panoply of human possibilities and misfortunes? Recall the French critic Charles du Bos' judgment of *War and Peace*: "Life would speak thus if life could speak."

To those who have been able to follow my reasoning thus far and can agree that prayer is fundamentally a radical response to life, it will be clear that one's choice of literature and of study material, of autobiographies and of theater, of movies and of sculpture to behold, is not an appendage to a "religious life" running parallel that calls for a weekly obligation called worship. The fruits of a deeply spiritual life are always a wholistic personality—schizophrenia of a spiritual kind is probably the most current affliction in believing circles—whereas there is, objectively speaking, no greater insult to the message of the Incarnation. If we can honestly and deeply believe that the Word became flesh, uniting all mankind and the cosmos, how can we at the same time insist on separating life as lived and experienced from graced life?

When we say that the arts are a means and more than a means

8. J.W.N. Sullivan, *Beethoven: His Spiritual Development* (New York: Vintage Books, 1927), p. 152.

9. In Henri Troyat, *Tolstoy* (New York: Dell, 1969), p. 349.

for becoming radical responders to life (and therefore a prayer-ful people), we mean, of course, that they may be such. It is necessary that their condition be subjected to criticism. Has the marketing mentality so imbued American consciousness that even the arts—and a fortiori life itself—are reduced to being another symbol for one's status rather than a beautiful experience to enjoy? Has the "Andy Hardy syndrome," which instructs us that poorer classes look askance at the arts, been with us so long that we have begun to believe that the poor are less capable of appreciating the arts (or of becoming artists) than the privileged classes? Must our culture continue to systematically exclude the poor from attending the theater, museums, symphonies? Is it not time that creative (as opposed to commercial) use of television bring authentic art to more and more viewers? And, what is more, to educe art from the numerous potential artists in every class of our culture?

The arts are the possession of all who care to live and live fully. The forests and rivers and oceans belong to all men, as do the great works of music and painting and cinema. No one owns Shakespeare's works. No prince's gate or castle wall can prevent us any longer from entering and enjoying, of being changed and sharing, what rightfully belongs to all. What can be said of a society's priorities when its national budget spends $6,000 on military hardware for every dollar spent on the arts?

The American temptation to project value on an object by pricing it has made most persons believe that the artist is the successful seller of his or her wares. But art refuses to be prostituted for long. Every person harbors within himself or herself the artist's vocation to create, whether that be expressed in one's love for cooking or sewing, for dancing or loving, for story-telling or mechanical repairing. To encourage the artist in another is to create a spirit-filled community. That old American nemesis, competition, has no place in the arts as such.

MUSIC AND SPIRITUALITY

For the sake of illustrating the powers of the arts for rooting and uprooting our life attitudes let us consider music's power to render us vulnerable. Our roots are so often laid bare to us when we listen to music, as Schopenhauer prophesied a century ago when he predicted that "only music reveals the irrational to modern man."

Music responds to life and its mysteries, as, for example, to the mystery of evil. For a Beethoven or a Gustav Mahler evil is an experience, not a philosophical concept, and for this reason we share the same mystery when we listen to their musical response that they tasted, swallowed, digested, and endured daily. Beethoven, whose busts adorn our comfortable museums and concert halls today, was no stranger to suffering and inconvenience during his lifetime. Loneliness stalked him to his death. His greatest gift, his sense of hearing, was poisoned so that deafness ate at his body and soul to the extent that when he directed his exaltent Ninth Symphony he had to be turned around at its end to see the applause of the audience that he could not hear. Despair was Beethoven's bed partner, but he never did forsake his root belief in life, as indicated in a letter to his friend, Dr. Wegler: "Oh, it is so beautiful to live—to live a thousand times!" Who can experience his Seventh Symphony and not feel he has been present at a great exultation of life for its own sake? Who can listen to the *Grosse Fugue* and not relive with Beethoven his personal acquaintance with suffering and evil?

Like Beethoven, Mahler had a firsthand acquaintance with the stranger Evil. He was the second of twelve children, and as a child he saw seven of his brothers and sisters die. His father was a tyrant who refused to support his family but did not hesitate to beat the children. By the time Gustav was twenty-nine both his parents were dead and his oldest brother had

committed suicide, and he took it upon himself to provide for
the children who remained. He lost his much-loved first daughter at four years of age and faced death for the last four years
of his life when doctors warned him he would die young of a
weak heart (in fact, he died at fifty from streptococcus, never
having listened to his final two symphonies).

When a friend heard Mahler's autobiographical Sixth Symphony for the first time he asked him: "How could a man as
kindhearted as you have written a symphony so full of bitter-
ness?" And Mahler replied: "It is the sum of all the suffering I
have been compelled to endure at the hands of life." In a conversation with his friend Bruno Walter, Mahler discusses what
his music means to him: "On what dark subsoil our life is built!
Whence do we come? Where does the way out lead? Why do
I believe myself free and yet wedged into my character as into
a prison? What is the purpose of suffering? How can I understand cruelty and malice in the creation of a kind God? Will the
meaning of life finally be revealed in death?" With all his personal familiarity with the mystery of evil, Mahler, like Beethoven, would not give up hope. "What a man makes of himself—
what he becomes through his untiring efforts to live and to be
—is permanent."[10]

From these brief explorations into the spiritual experience—
the life-responses of just two significant musicians—we learn
something of the source of the musical response to life. It is no
wonder that music renders listeners so vulnerable to life's roots
and fulfills William James's analysis that music and not conceptual speech "is the element through which we are best spoken
to by mystical truth. . . . There is a verge of the mind which
these things haunt. . . . It alone has the keeping of the password
primeval"(322).

But music's spiritual power is not restricted to its mystical or

10. Cited in Alma Mahler, *Gustav Mahler: Memories and Letters* (Seattle:
University of Washington Press, 1968), pp. 260f.

psychological rooting. Music uproots as well, as Plato sensed when he warned that "when modes of music change, the fundamental laws of the State always change with them."[11] Mahler's personal torments and wrestlings with despair anticipated by fifty years the anxieties and aspirations of the hundreds of thousands who today flock to hear his music performed. He shattered the suprarational and superficially optimistic biases of the enlightenment culture of the nineteenth century, and in doing so finds ready listeners in an atomic age America, where science and a shallow belief in man's goodness have been shattered by truth-bearing events. Like two other of his countrymen, Sigmund Freud and Franz Kafka, Mahler "sensed in the early years of our century the immanent upheavals in Western civilization."[12]

The prophetic power of music is especially conspicuous in recent American cultural happenings. One considers, for example, the so-called "Negro spiritual": "To the uninformed listener the words spoke of religious longing; . . . to the viewer all was piety and submission. The true meaning of the spirituals, however, involves a communication from one to another regarding plans for escape, hostile feelings toward the master, and a general expression of rebellious attitudes" (Grier, 123). Would there be a Black Power movement today without the spirituals and jazz, spiritual precursors that paved the way for political pride and creativity? Would the black man possess the soul to seek justice for himself if it had not been carved out and deepened by his exposure to despair through his music?

The youth movement of modern America is inconceivable apart from its music. Elvis Presley in the fifties threw off a Cartesian corporeal hangup (a white youth problem, not one for blacks); the Beatles carried on with a mystical rock beat that

11. *The Republic* (Book 4), in *The Dialogues of Plato*, Jowett, trans. (New York: Random House, 1937), p. 424.
12. Davie Hall, as cited in Herbert Reid, "Mahler and the Modern Temper," notes to *Mahler Symphony No. 2 in C Minor* (Columbia Recording: M2S 695).

appealed to youth in diverse cultures the world over and opened the door for active participation and creation by numerous other groups. America's social protests of the sixties (and therefore of the seventies) derived their life-blood from Bob Dylan's "The Times They Are A-Changin' " (the movement's anthem); Peter, Paul, and Mary's "If I Had a Hammer" (to say nothing of "Rich Man, Poor Man"); Joan Baez' protest songs, one of which is dedicated to the four children killed in Birmingham, Alabama, on September 15, 1963, "Birmingham Sunday":

> Come around by my side and I'll sing you a song
> I'll sing it so softly, it will do no one wrong
> On Birmingham Sunday, the blood ran like wine,
> And the choir kept singing of freedom.
>
> On Birmingham Sunday, the noise shook the ground
> And people all over the earth turned around,
> For no one recalled a more cowardly sound
> And the choir kept singing of freedom.

There is nothing obtuse or mistaken about the position on social justice that these singers take, whether tackling the question of racism, war, or economic injustices. Nor is there predicting their effect on a generation of youth raised on this prophetic music, though one thing is clear: The reception the current generation gives its musicians suggests that this generation, so attuned to music, may be as spiritually minded—that is, as primarily interested in human life for its own sake—as any generation in history. And this not by accident but by—if one must find a single cause—technology, which, through the media no less than through the mountains of cassettes, recorders, stereos, and amplifiers, has provided a generation of youth on several continents with mystical and prophetic music at their finger tips. This positive contribution of technology is sorely missed by many European mystics (one thinks of Heidegger and Marcel) to say nothing of American ones (Roszak seems overly rigid in his hatred for technology here).

Adolescence is the primary period in a person's history for developing his or her powers of mysticism. The invasion of record shops by rivers of eager young shoppers, the hours passed listening to music in preference to reading books, is not idle time. Music has proven to be the place where a young adult most often plants his mystical and prophetic roots. Music becomes a spiritual temple, the place of ecstacy and of wonder as well as of battle and of warfare with life and its usurpers.

While all music (and we are talking of good music) need not be prayer, all of it may be—and very often is when it is engaged in, whether by composer, musician, director, or listener, as a radical response to life. What we have said about music applies to all the arts: to poetry, to painting, to sculpture, to architecture, to movies, to dance, to the theater, to novels (their authorship as much as their reading), to sport. Where human life and its mysteries are engaged for their own sake and enjoyed for their own sake and where effort is made to share this gift more broadly, there is the Spirit breathing "unutterable groans beseeching God for us."

The Arts and Spiritualities When we propose that the arts can in fact be the place for authentic prayer, we are exposing a sensitive nerve that has divided western Christian spiritualities for centuries. One can recognize in western spiritualities two divergent schools: the negative (those who consider the experience of nothingness to be ultimate for a spirituality) and the positive (I prefer the term humanist, for these people consider that all the world is already God-made and God-given and that therefore an experience of the possibilities of man and creation can be an authentic starting point for a spirituality). The negativists tend to define history as what began with Christ, while the humanists sense that Christ's coming was but a special moment in a continually unfolding act of creation.

To grasp the historical setting for a humanistic Christian

spirituality, let me trace some of the battle lines erected regarding Christian attitudes toward music. Jesus seemed to have no difficulty with music, making his presence felt at festivals and marriage banquets, suggesting that "the rocks and the stones would sing" and calling out to his detractors that "we pipe to you and you do not dance." The early Christian gatherings, which were in homes, invariably broke into "hymns and sacred songs."

The negativists raised their voices in shrill protest in the fourth and fifth centuries (pessimistic ones especially in the West as the "barbarians were coming") in the person of Chrysostom in the eastern church: "lest demons introducing lascivious songs should overthrow everything God established the psalms"; and Augustine in the West: "The Christian musician is a member of two worlds, the spiritual and the material. The choice is his; to create sacred music that is pleasing to God because it ennobles character or to defile the miracle of creation and produce secular music which arouses lust and desire." Note that, in additon to the segregation of the sacred and the secular in these commentators, we also have an emphasis on sexual lust as a (in fact, *the*) most grievous offense to the deity. We have here a psychologizing of reality: spiritual evil is within oneself and the cure for it is self-control and self-discipline. In this context the *political* appears to be ignored (it can never be done away with, however, and surfaces at the most inopportune moments); music as prophecy is not only discouraged but is, most probably, feared by these spiritual writers, bent as they were on integrating Christian and imperial powers (cf. Augustine's *City of God*). They fear the destructive, the No power, of music as being inimical to the power of the State, not unlike Plato sensed that music would presage political upheavals.

The rather short-lived secularization of western Christianity in the twelfth century as well as its renaissance in the thirteenth were in great part inspired by musicians who, wandering through the countryside of southern France singing their love songs or through Italian villages intoning their *laudi spirituali*, ushered in the vernacular languages. The emergence of local languages presaged the birth of multiple cultures within Christendom that we today designate as nations of Europe. The musician ushered in a spiritual movement inspired by Francis of Assisi (who took up the music as he did the life-style of the lower classes); Dominic, a perambulatory singer (who turned his attention to the newly found universities); and Thomas Aquinas, who wrote music and poetry, claimed that "Christ is music," and spent a lifetime marrying the newly discovered works of Greek and Arabic thinkers with Jewish and Christian traditions. His books were publicly burned in Paris because his humanistic spirituality was too great a threat to the guardians of the status quo, constructed as it was on a negative spiritual premise.

The fourteenth century, with the Black Plague decimating 30 percent of the population, was a field day for apocalyptic and negative spiritual writers who sought to withdraw from the marriage of society and the sacred. The beginnings of the Renaissance in the sixteenth century touched Martin Luther, prophetic spirit that he was, to an appreciation of music for music's sake. "Music is a beautiful, gracious gift of God," and "God preaches the Gospel through music" (*Eulogy of Music*). Calvin, on the other hand, returned to Augustine's negative spirituality, and the artistic iconoclasm that characterized much of the Protestant enthusiastic sects is well known. (In many cases, for example, the Puritans or the Quakers, this apparent iconoclasm may well have been a heightened prophetic—i.e., political—consciousness, but this is not the place to pursue this historical matter further.) On the Catholic side, the Council of Trent forbade "exaggerated" polyphony in the sixteenth century. This condemnation has been said to symbolize the gradual withdrawal of the churches, both Protestant and Catholic, from "worldly" post-Renaissance music (Portnoy, 159).

At this time the printing press accomplished a veritable revo-

lution in music, allowing for the easier, cheaper, and broader
distribution of musical scores and autographs, allowing the lay
musician at least some autonomy and power. Music was beginning to be democratized, and with it a spirituality that rendered
ineffective the priggish and aristocratic spirituality Santayana
complains contemplation had become since Aristotle, for whom
"contemplative activity is almost synonymous with talkative
leisure and the progression of science; as if a wanderer, a singer,
a saint, or a child could not be as contemplative as a philosopher."[13] The Church at its organizational level invoked a negative spirituality, encouraging a turtlelike withdrawal into a
cloistered world buttressed by the religion-art dichotomy of a
Chrysostom or an Augustine. As the divorce between aesthetic
and religious experience became more and more pronounced
one might hear pleas from pious prelates to "get religion back
into the arts"—as if the faith and despair, sin and passion, that
drove the artist to compose were not the very stuff of the Spirit.
A rational dichotomy and rigid distinction between the aesthetic and religious experience, clung to by believers who trust
their faith so little that they must project their weaknesses on
the rest of mankind, does not hold in the spiritual lives and
struggles of growing numbers of Americans who seek their
authentic vocation as a contemplative one: that is, as a synthetic
process of realizing an over-all meaning and value to life and
their daily activities.

It is significant how lay-oriented and unclerical is musical
spirituality. The great musicians have been proclaimed saints
by the human race—one thinks of Mozart, Beethoven, Bach as
examples—while the clerical world preoccupied itself with vy-
ing to raise funds necessary to canonize this obscure member
of a religious order or that monk who spent his life in a monastery. The spiritual giants of the world we inhabit—the great

13. "Apropos of Aristotle," in *Animal Faith and Spiritual Life*, ed. John Lachs
(New York: Appleton-Century-Crofts, 1967), p. 304.

persons of prayer who responded to life radically—are very often the musicians who endured extreme poverty and misery in the process of being true to their vocations and who, by their gifts and their dedication, continue to draw hundreds of thousands of souls into realms where they may respond to life radically. The failure of the churches to engage western man spiritually in the last three centuries is nowhere more evident than in the fact that one can say without fear of contradiction that Mozart's spiritual influence on the West has exceeded that of all the saints canonized since the Renaissance.

We have traced the spiritual history of music alone, but a similar story would hold for the relation of western Christian spiritualities to other arts and artists as well, for art is the natural vehicle for nurturing and encouraging the mystic and the prophet in every adult. Americans are invited to resist the myth that the appreciation of art requires money (or its institutionalized equivalent, years of education). What art requires is love and the poor are at least as rich in that as the wealthy. Nor do the arts require money to justify their existence. The arts, like the mysteries of life they communicate, belong to everyone who cares to feel and hear, see and touch, suffer and be moved. When a people begin to receive beauty for its own sake they are becoming a spiritual people, as Mahler testified near the end of his life. "All creation adorns itself continually for God. Everyone therefore has only one duty, to be as beautiful as possible in every way in the eyes of God and man. Ugliness is an insult to God." (in Mahler, 168)

Postscript: A Fresh Look at the Trinity

In the Introduction to this reflection on the contemporary spiritual situation, I proposed that we must search out the simple that has been lost if we are to reconstruct our shattered spiritual lives. A return to the simple implies standing once again before life to feel, touch, and experience: to share it, to celebrate, and to allow life to affect us, evoking our prayer. It implies putting life first—and this means all other concerns, including security, status, ego trips of all stripes, come second. A spiritual person is one for whom life holds priority over all else, including life's mediators. Where life is sought for its own sake lies the spiritual.

We have identified today's prayer as a *root, or radical, response to life and its mysteries.* If our basic attitude toward life is grasped as a calling to become rooted (to enjoy simply to enjoy) and to uproot (to confront injustice simply because it is there)—and in a real sense that is *all* life is about; it is our only duty in life—then our prayer life becomes a life lived at this depth or root level. Adult prayer is nothing if it is not life lived on a level of mysticism and prophecy. And a life lived at a deepening level of mysticism and prophecy *is* a life of adult prayer. I believe that today more and more persons are preparing to respond to this adult vocation; to hear its call first of all. To leave behind a childish religion for adult faith is to cast out into uncharted seas (for if they were already charted, human history would read far differently from the bleak and repetitively cruel saga that it does). Spiritual adults must stand together as a people in support of one another; not only because we are each too weak to long endure individually, but especially because it is more fun that way.

In exploring the meaning of spirituality today and its essence, prayer, we have inadvertently stumbled across an insight into Trinitarian belief. This was in no way a goal or conscious expectation of this study, though it is curious that the Trinity as an experience and not as a dogma was the only avenue by which a Trinitarian belief arose in the first few centuries of Christian believers. Our insight has occurred in a similarly experiential fashion. What I have in mind is best illustrated by a diagram:

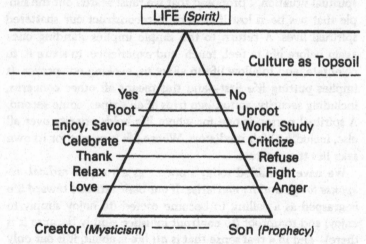

The Spirit, life itself, is the ultimate gift. Life is tenuous and the roots it requires for survival sink deeper than topsoil which is one's culture. The probing of these deep roots is in the direction of mysticism and prophecy, symbolized by Father and Son. The Father represents our Yes response to life because the gift of life is always intended to be *enjoyed* by its giver: the pleasure of future generations is always the dream of any father as father. The Son, who represents our No by fighting to share life, is a prophet in the long line of Jewish and other Near Eastern prophets before his time and since his murder. But he is more than a prophet (as any authentic prophet is); he is also a radical lover, a receiver of life at its roots from his Father. Thus, to paraphrase Gunter Grass, "wrapped up mysteriously like an enigma in his No there lies hidden a Yes." And within every Yes there is inferred a No. This is why the Father cannot do without the Son, nor the Son without the Father.

Their dual direction of life-response remains coiled in constant tension. Yet this dialectic persists as the sole support for the Spirit, the gift of life. Our spiritual adulthood is learning to live with the tension, knowing that it alone allows life to breathe and be passed on. Like a coiled spring, there hides a power here bigger than ourselves, capable of carrying us beyond ourselves and thereby upholding life, so long as we allow both poles of the dialectic a full place in our lives, not concentrating on one pole at the expense of the other. Our Yes needs to be Yes; and our No, No.

This Trinitarian experience, with its tension between enjoying life and sharing it, and which so many of us feel personally and socially today, is a far cry from the three-leaf clovers, the three in one and one in three mathematical games and the substance-person-nature subtleties of Greek philosophical categories by which we were introduced to the Trinity. Yet, just as the Greek treatment of the Trinity was for the Greeks of the fourth century a deeply felt experience, one that provoked society to rioting in the streets and to riding bishops out of town on rails, so too this Trinitarian experience is provocative. The centuries-long battle over *filioque* is no longer a hollow polemic of propositions but arouses contemporary consciences into facing the constant temptation of religion: that of becoming so comfortable in its mysticism that prophecy (the Son) becomes too untidy a route (and therefore a secondary route) for the Spirit to travel through human history.

A return to a living belief (i.e., one that *affects* our places and manner of life, our priorities and our attitudes) in this Trinity;

a return to an authentic praise of the Spirit which is life: this is one of the few promises of the many beckoning mankind currently that is simple enough to ring true, historical enough to attract, powerful enough to effect change. If we can entertain this promise in a personal way, making it our own by common discussion and living of it, then we will dare to say No where we must today. And from the No of today will be born the Yes of tomorrow.

If our reunderstanding of prayer in some way mirrors what is actually happening in the opening minds, bodies, and hearts of alive (i.e., spiritual) persons today, then consequences for spirituality follow from it. As we noted in the Introduction, to alter one's understanding of prayer even slightly is to change the whole course of one's life, for in dealing with prayer we are treating the heart of spirituality. I suggest, for example, the following reunderstanding of basic spiritual terms, though their fuller meanings and consequences must be explored elsewhere: Prayer: a radical response to life. Spirituality: one's attitude toward life or consciousness. Faith: an abiding trust that life is a gift. Grace: the ever-present gift, and gifts, of life. Sacrament: social celebration of a particular mystery of life. Church: a place (i.e., a people) where life is responded to radically. In our time, as in other periods of intense cultural upheaval, the Spirit is blowing where it wills and not necessarily through the departments to which bureaucratic man would assign it. Our reception and response to the Spirit is the new spirituality, for better or for worse.

About the Author

A visionary activist, and one of the most important religious thinkers and teachers of our time, Matthew Fox has devoted his career to unleashing the suppressed mystical and life-affirming traditions within Christianity and other faiths. His theology of "Creation Spirituality"—the belief that we are born in "original blessing"—has reinvigorated the faith of countless seekers and earned him the headline-making censure of the Vatican, which officially "silenced" Fox in 1989 and precipitated his dismissal by the Dominican Order in 1993. Now an Episcopal priest, Fox is the author of more than twenty books, including *Original Blessing; One River, Many Wells,* and *The Coming of the Cosmic Christ.* He is founding president of the University of Creation Spirituality in Oakland, California. In 1995, Fox was awarded The Peace Abbey Courage of Conscience Award. Recently, Fox has been nationally praised for his groundbreaking "techno cosmic masses," which combine the world's faiths in a reconstruction of liturgical celebration embracing dance, techno music, and multimedia. He lives in California.

For more information about the work of Matthew Fox and the master's degree in creation spirituality offered at Naropa Oakland and the Doctor of Ministry degree at the University of Creation Spirituality in Oakland, California, call 510-835-4827 or consult the following web site: www.creationspirituality.com